Colouring
Techniques for
Woodturners

Colouring
Techniques for
Woodturners

Jan Sanders

Guild of Master Craftsman Publications Ltd

First published 1996 by
Guild of Master Craftsman Publications Ltd,
166 High Street, Lewes,
East Sussex BN7 1XU

© Jan Sanders 1996

Reprinted 2000

ISBN 1 86108 009 3

Photography © John Sanders 1996

Illustrations © John Yates 1996

Designed by Teresa Dearlove

Typeface: Cheltenham

Printed and bound in Singapore under the supervision of
MRM Graphics, Winslow, Bucks, UK
Colour separation by Viscan Graphics, Singapore

Acknowledgements

I would like to thank:

My dear friend Jean Hopkins for her unlimited patience, encouragement and genuine interest in reorganising my literary imperfections, and for engaging Cheryl Morgan, who so efficiently typed the script for me; my husband John, who took all the photographs for the book, and has been a tremendous support, offering practical advice and encouragement at every stage; Liz Inman and Jonathan Ingoldby, my editors at GMC Publications; my family, and all those friends, many of them woodturners, from whom I received offers of help and encouragement while writing this book.

To my dear John, without whose inexhaustible enthusiasm and persistence, this book would still be just an idea.

Contents

Introduction

I have always had a love for the countryside and the natural world, and this led in turn to an interest in traditional crafts. I began with straw plaiting and corn dolly making, and then moved on to become a professional willow-basket maker.

The traditional forms of design involved in this craft and the wonderful colours which nature provided – ranging from the dark green-brown of natural willow wands to the fresh creamy white of stripped, newly cut rods – gave me tremendous pleasure and satisfaction, and at that time I had no desire to extend the colour range of my work using dyes of any kind.

However, some time later, my husband introduced me to woodturning, and I served an invaluable apprenticeship with him, beginning by roughing out cord pulls. As my technical skills matured, so did my interest in design, which led me to develop my own ideas. At the same time, John was encouraging me to experiment with colour to add a further dimension to my work.

My first attempts were tentative, but each one encouraged me to move forward and experiment with ever bolder colour combinations. I found that adding colour to my work opened up a fascinating new dimension to my turning, and I have never looked back.

The colouring of turned work has received relatively little attention, although the decoration of wood by the application of colour is not a new concept. For centuries, wood

has been coloured by craftspeople using naturally occurring dyes and pigments. Today, modern technology is aiding us in reviving and developing ancient skills in wood decoration, and these can readily be applied to turnery.

The reason for colouring wood remains the same today as in the past: to enhance its visual appeal. This is especially the case with the plainer-grained woods which can be greatly enhanced by the addition of colour dye.

There are many different products which the woodturner can use to colour wood, and a variety of methods of applying them to create different effects. Once you have mastered the basic techniques of woodcolouring, you will find that there is no limit to the potential for innovative creativity and diverse, beautiful finishes.

Little has been written about colouring turned wood with dye, so the emphasis of this book is entirely on turned work, although all the finishes I have used do have wider applications, such as colouring flat work, and restoring furniture and picture frames.

Always remember that colour will not make up for a poor design, and is never intended to hide bad workmanship. The aim of colouring with dye is not to paint the piece into oblivion, but to enhance its natural beauty. At its highest level, such work can be elevated to an artistic plane where it can stand alongside fine ceramics and glassware.

Opposite top
Turned shapes ready for colouring . . .
Opposite below
. . . and after colouring.

Inspiration and design: marrying colours and shapes

To me, there is no more beautiful a sight than a mature tree standing majestic in its summer foliage. It combines strength, beauty, form and colour. It is a natural work of art.

Woodturners, however, will generally be more interested in the wood than the tree. Strangely though, once wood has been turned, many woodturners seem reluctant to favour it with some of the colours which surrounded it in its natural environment; not just the

3

green of the leaves or the brown of the bark, but the blues and other multiple hues of the sky at sunrise, sunset, twilight and even at night, or the colours of the flowers which grew around it.

The natural world offers a wealth of ideas, from the multiple colours of the rainbow to the subtle grey tones of a seascape. I often record scenes and other images which are sources of inspiration for colour in my designs, using my sketch book or camera. These are filed, together with additional notes, for future reference. I have also found that man-made sources of colour such as pillar boxes and pianos can provide inspiration.

Below and right
The natural world offers a wealth of inspiration for colouring. I used this photograph of the boat on the water as the basis for colouring this elm platter. The wild grain formation led me to use the grain-guided colouring technique (see Chapter 10) to achieve the effect you see here.

Consider also the way in which use of colour can impart a sense of balance to a piece. I frequently have dark and light coloured sides on my pedestals to convey a contrast of, say, day and night. Equally, the use of dark colours at the base of a piece impart the effect of stability and solidity, while paler colours at the top give a piece a delicate, floating appearance. A pattern which flows up from the base gives a piece an uplifting impression, whereas a similar pattern painted down from the top will have the reverse effect. Dark colours such as browns, dark greens and black can impart a sombre feel to a piece, while bright yellows, delicate greens and pale blues are more refreshing and uplifting.

Although the choice of colour in the end is very subjective, in some cases it can be objective too. Perhaps the items in question are toys, in which case their users – children – will be naturally attracted to bright colours. Coloured toys are educational, too, as they can be related directly to other everyday things and teach children their colours.

If the turned items are to be coloured and given as presents, then it may be helpful to take your cue from the established decor of the house or room in which they are going to live. Ask yourself if the piece would benefit from a related figurative or abstract design painted on it instead of, or as well as, an overall complimentary colour dye.

Above
Bright yellows and blues give a refreshing and uplifting impression. You can also see here how a limited range of colours in different combinations can be used to create striking effects.
Below
Sunset platter. The combination of colour and shape, and the variety these can lend to a design, is extremely wide ranging. Use your imagination and experiment!

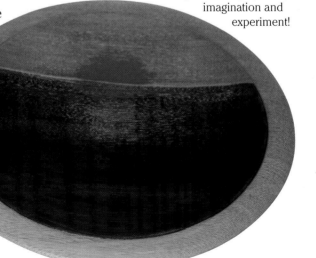

These same considerations must obviously be given great attention where a piece is specifically commissioned for decoration or for use in a particular setting. This would usually be chosen in conjunction with the client, so a pooling of ideas would hopefully lead to a choice of colour for the piece that would compliment its surroundings.

With only a limited range of dye colours, you can create striking effects on your work. The combination of colour and shape, and the variety these aspects can lend to a design, is wide ranging, and experimenting can be a lot of fun! This book will, I hope, set you firmly on your way.

Colouring can bring infinite interest
and variety to a single form.

CHAPTER 1

Shapes for colouring

L et us look for a moment at the different categories of turned work and the sort of items they embrace. The following list will also hold the interest of the non-turner in sifting through the possibilities of obtaining pieces for colouring.

Categories of turning

Small domestic

Breadboards, egg-cups, scoops, pestle and mortars, salad/fruit bowls, goblets, candleholders, cord pulls and bottle coasters.

Household furniture

Side tables, stools, plant stands, curtain poles and finials, mirrors, standard/table lamps and cradles.

Antique restoration and reproduction work

Spindles in great variety for tables, chairs, cupboards, dressers, door and drawer knobs, overmantels.

Architectural

Pillars, columns, stair rails, balusters, finials and plinths.

Artistic shapes

One-off inspirational pieces including multi-section pieces, off-centre turning and barley twist techniques.

When looking for shapes to colour from within the categorised groups, remember that dye and colour effects are embellishments, so a complex design is not always necessary. In fact, it is far better to err on the side of simplicity, especially to begin with, as this limits the number of angles of grain to cope with when trying to get an even coverage of dye or stain. Later on, beads, coves, Vs and finials will provide profiles for special effects.

When making your own sketches with either form or colouring in mind, it is a useful tip to draw a line from top to bottom on the page of your sketch book and draw half the design, using the line as the centre axis of the piece. Fold the paper along the line and then cut around the outline using scissors or a scalpel. You will then have a sample of the total profile of your idea. Few people can draw both sides of a profile to match – I know I can't – so I frequently use this system to judge whether a design for a piece will actually 'work' (see Fig 1.1). If you don't want to cut the designs out, then use transparent paper for the exercise and trace through one half on to the other. Even the design of an item as small as a cord pull can benefit from a few preliminary sketches, particularly as they have a specific function which must be taken into account in advance (see Fig 1.2).

Fig 1.1
When designing the profiles of your designs, you will find it extremely helpful to draw a line down the centre of your sketch pad and draw only half the design. The paper can then be folded over and the design cut out, providing you with an accurate symmetrical shape.

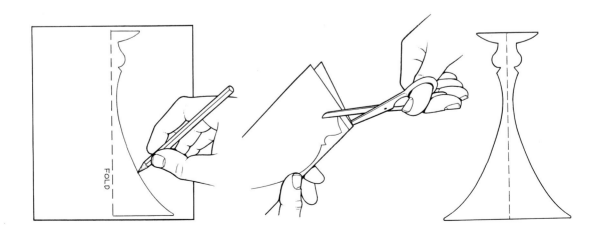

Fig 1.2
Cord pulls in different designs,
before and after colouring.

To me, the different shapes and functions of turned work suggest various ways to colour and use colouring effects. Here are some examples which might help you as an initial guide on choosing shapes to colour.

Salad bowl

I recommend only colouring the outside of a salad bowl to avoid the possibility of the colour coming into contact with food. Even if the colour is food safe, the food may spoil the colour! The design calls for a clear demarcation between the inside and outside of the bowl as far as the colour is concerned. Refer to Fig 1.3: you may choose to turn a flat rim with a clean edge to it (a), or a beaded rim (b). In both cases, the colour would stop below the outside top of the rim.

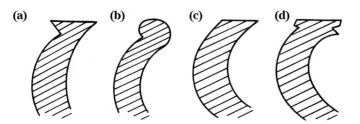

Fig 1.3
Rim designs for a salad bowl.

A rim like (c), which would be dyed to the upper outside edge, stands a good chance of the dye creeping along the grain across the flat surface of the rim, marring the appearance. If you decide to colour the rim alone, careful brushwork is needed to prevent the dye from spoiling the interior of the bowl. Cutting a fine V helps to create a physical as well as a visual demarcation line, as shown in (d).

Candleholders

When making candleholders for colouring, again simplicity in design is the essence of success. Fig 1.4 shows three suggestions which give an uncluttered profile on which to colour.

Fig 1.4
Three possible design suggestions for candleholders.

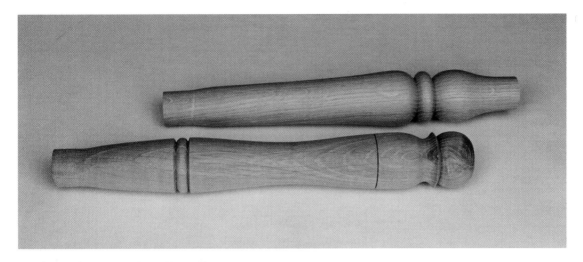

Fig 1.5
Two oak legs showing different profiles, and the undercut seat for a three-legged stool. After colouring you could consider filling the V cuts with liming or patinating wax to create extra interest.

Stool

A three-legged stool is easier to make than a four-legged stool, and saves the worry of getting it to stand evenly! However, three legged stools are not recommended for standing on – remember they were originally made to sit on while milking a cow! Their simple shapes, often using branch wood for the legs, were never coloured.

Forgetting its original use, but keeping a country look, we can now afford to upgrade both the construction and design, adding colour and even a special effect to enhance the piece.

For example, I would suggest adding a bit of shape to the legs to create some interest and contour for liming or patinating, and perhaps a narrow V on the undercut seat which can also be limed (see Fig 1.5).

Above **Fig 1.6**
Two vase designs, coloured and uncoloured. Such shapes lend themselves to the application of many colouring techniques and special effects.
Below **Fig 1.7**
Designs can be reflective of mood.

Vases

These are a favourite form of mine, and you will see many examples in this book. As with candleholders, balance and simplicity contribute greatly to a successful and aesthetically pleasing design. You can see from Fig 1.6 how such shapes lend themselves to a wide variety of colouring techniques and special effects. Their balanced shape means that they are also acceptable upside-down!

A design can be reflective of a mood. The vase on the left of Fig 1.7 illustrates a 'sad' countenance by virtue of the downturned mouth, whereas the vase on the right appears cheerful by virtue of the upturned mouth.

Antique restoration and reproduction work

Both require the use of many dyes and stains from the wood colour range, mainly to provide a match with the previously dyed wood in old furniture or simulating the same in new pieces (see Fig 1.8). Occasionally, light coloured paints may be required to match those used on the original piece. In this instance the shapes for colouring and the colours are copies of the originals. Picture frames and overmantels frequently need restoration using one of the variety of gilt products and, although they require no turning, they do require the application of colouring techniques which are covered in this book.

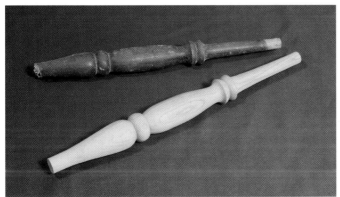

(a)

Fig 1.8
Modern dyes and stains are frequently used to simulate the look of old wood in restored pieces of furniture. Here you can see how effective careful staining can be, when you compare the new, unfinished spindle in (a) with the coloured and finished spindle in (b).

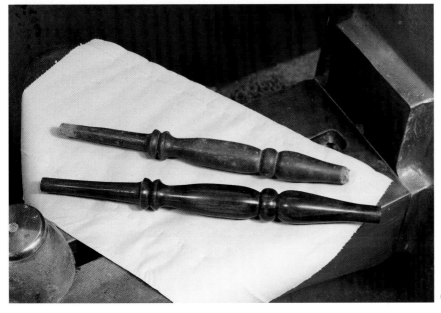

(b)

Architectural turning

The colouring of architectural turning is frequently done to commission, and often to simulate another medium. For instance, a pillar may be required to look like marble or cracked plaster. Larger items may be required to match their surroundings or other woodwork and so call for the application of dyes or paints. A project which is likely to be undertaken by the hobby turner might be making a new set of stair rails, newels and finials. Dyeing these anything from dark mahogany to a pastel shade, or with a white stain, can make a huge difference to the ambience of a stairwell.

This is another case where drawing half the profile on folded paper and cutting out can assist enormously in creating a pleasing design. You may even find that the negative form is actually more pleasing than the positive one. Every time you draw one profile you are really drawing two!

Fig 1.9
The inspiration for this piece was a kingfisher diving into a lily pond. The piece is 12in (305mm) in diameter.

Fig 1.10
'Raindrops'. This piece is 20in
(508mm) high and the leaf is 14in
(356mm) in diameter.

Artistic shapes

Artistic shapes for colouring are, by definition, created
with colouring firmly in mind at the design stage.

I regard artistic shapes as being individually designed
and created by the originator, to the extent that if they are
copied then it is perfectly obvious that this has been the
case. To achieve individuality, it is extremely helpful, but
by no means essential, to have a source of inspiration.
For the example of artistic turning shown in Fig 1.9, the
design and colour are part and parcel of the complete
representation. The inspirational source for this piece
was a kingfisher diving into a lily pond.

The piece entitled 'Raindrops' comes from my water lily
series. The spent seed pod of the lily flower is depicted
using a banksia cone, which is supported above the leaf.
The blending of blue and yellow on the two opposite sides
of the piece represents the contrast between a sunny day
and the darkness of evening. The floating leaf is supported
by a yellow pedestal symbolising air bubbles rising from
the depths of the lily pond (see Fig 1.10).

Artistic turning as a subject is almost inexhaustible,
and merits a volume in its own right.

CHAPTER 2

Materials and equipment

Although there are many products on the market which are suitable for use in colouring wood, not all are necessarily suitable for use on turned work, and some products are easier to apply than others. I will be concentrating on a selection of ready-prepared items which can be used successfully by anyone new to colouring, in the hope that this will give you the confidence to explore the field further.

Proprietary products use many of the components which have been used traditionally, some of which have been updated by substituting synthetic substances for the old organic ones. In many cases, this has improved the handling and, consequently, the finish.

Suppliers' catalogues provide comprehensive lists of products to choose from, and the range can be extremely bewildering. What to choose? Where to start?

Abrasives

The use of the correct abrasive is of paramount importance in achieving an appropriate standard of finish prior to dyeing. The final preparation of a piece will require three or four increasingly fine grades of abrasive: say 120, 180 and 240, finishing with 320 grit, and finally grade 0000 steel wool (see Fig 2.1).

Fig 2.1
A selection of abrasives, including grade 0000 steel wool.

For the majority of my work, I prefer to use fabric-backed abrasives. Although these can vary in quality, they are generally very good and much more pliable than the card-backed variety. This is a great advantage, in that it allows them to follow the profile of a piece without creasing. For areas where this flexibility is too great, such as beads or Vs, you can easily support the abrasive with a piece of card.

Tack cloth

Tack cloths are made from a muslin which contains resinous substances designed to pick up dust particles off the surface of the wood, leaving a clean surface on which to apply your chosen colour or finish.

I always follow the steel wool stage with a pass from the tack cloth, and you will find these two items used in partnership regularly in the process of colouring turned work.

Safety cloth

This is an extremely useful synthetic cloth used for polishing. It is designed so that, while it has the polishing properties of an ordinary cloth, it tears easily, like paper, making it extremely safe for use on revolving work where there is a risk of it getting caught (see Fig 2.2).

Colouring materials

Dyes, stains and many of the other products used in this book were originally developed for woodworkers and decorative finishers rather than woodturners. It is only relatively recently that some woodturners have 'borrowed' these products, and adapted them as necessary for specialist use.

Experienced colourists experiment with practically anything, from blackberry juice to Indian ink! However, if you are new to colouring you will find the selection of

Fig 2.2
Safety cloth has the polishing properties of ordinary cloth, but tears like paper, making it much safer to use on revolving work.

proprietary brands of dyes and stains extremely comprehensive and entirely adequate for your needs. Not that this should stop you from experimenting!

Choosing a colouring material

The criteria you should set yourself when choosing a colouring material should be:

- Suitability for the specific task.
- Ease of application.
- Effectiveness of finish.

These criteria incorporate colour response, drying times and compatibility of products.

Water-based dyes

Water-based dyes are the easiest to handle, and are obtainable in a wide range of colours from a variety of manufacturers. As manufacturers use different base materials in their products, their colours may vary slightly from one another. Water-based dyes are available either in ready to use liquid form, or as powder for dilution.

Acrylic water-based stains

Similar in properties to water-based dyes, these stains contain a substantial acrylic element which minimises the effects of grain raising (see page 54) and allows an even application of dye over large areas of dry wood, without overlap marks.

Acrylic stains are usually applied with sponge applicators, which are formed with a chisel edge for cutting in. This makes life much easier when dyeing up a bead, for instance, without colouring the bead itself, or for butting one colour up to another. These sponges are available in a variety of sizes; 1in (25mm), 2in (51mm), 3in (76mm) and so on. I usually buy them in pairs, one for applying the stain and the other for removing surplus stain from the work. This technique is described more fully on page 82.

Spirit-based dyes

Spirit dyes require more careful handling, as their absorption is more immediate. They come either ready to use or in concentrated liquid form.

Spirit- and water-based dyes are available in a range of wood colours, and what I will term 'spectrum' colours (usually variants of red, yellow, blue and green) (see Fig 2.3). Both spirit- and water-based dyes can be used to 'paint' or describe pictures or patterns on wood where the grain can remain visible. However, for opaque lines and effects, I find that artist's tempera or gouache paints provide the best coverage.

In addition, felt-tip pens which contain a range of spirit dyes have recently been developed for the woodworker. These are very useful for line painting, and also for touching-in small areas.

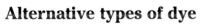

Fig 2.3
A selection of spirit- and water-based dyes and stains.

Alternative types of dye

As I have already indicated, there are many other prepared and natural dyes which can be used for colouring wood, apart from those specifically developed for the woodworker. So do try other colouring materials once you have gained some experience and confidence with proprietary dyes and stains. For example, Indian ink (useful for delicate patterns and drawings), felt-tip pens (useful for line drawing and touching-in), spirit-based leather dye (the darker colours can be particularly effective) and fabric dyes, which are available in a huge range of colours.

You could also consider using organic dyes, such as the blackberry juice mentioned earlier. One of the oldest known organic dyes is cochineal, a red food dye, which is in fact now manufactured synthetically and can be used to equal effect. Synthetic food dyes are also available in other, equally vibrant colours.

Car enamel and cellulose paints also have a place in colouring wood. However, such paints used alone will obliterate the grain and, as a result, I have not included them in the techniques and projects which follow, with the exception of ebonising (see Chapter 17).

Brushes

I find brushes better than sponge applicators for use with water- and spirit-based dyes. There are many specialist brushes available and the best way to choose them is to select a shape and size which is most suitable for the job in hand.

Brushes are made from various types of animal hair, such as sable, squirrel and ox, as well as from synthetic filaments. They can vary enormously in price, and the cheapest should be avoided if at all possible. They have short working lives and are inclined to shed hairs. Buy the best quality brushes you can afford. Providing they are washed carefully after use, they will provide sterling service.

To extend the life of brushes used with spirit dyes, be sure to clean with white spirit, and then wash thoroughly in warm soapy water. Rinse out, and stand up to dry naturally.

I make frequent use of square-edged oxhair flat lacquer brushes, which allow me to cut in easily and cleanly where a neat edge is required. For painting detailed designs or small areas such as rims and beads, I use round, pointed or square-ended squirrel or sable brushes, depending on which shape best fits the profile and size of the work I am colouring.

Fine-pointed brushes known as artist's pencil brushes are needed when painting patterns or pictures (see Chapter 11), and similar but round-ended brushes are useful when applying gilt varnish and fontenay

Fig 2.4
A selection of brushes, along with other essential equipment for painting: absorbent paper, sponge applicators with 'chisel edges', useful for cutting-in, jam jar of clean water, ceramic palette, general-purpose sponge, and a selection of brushes, stored upright after cleaning.

bases (see Chapter 18).

You will also need containers, such as jam jars, in which to wash your brushes on a regular basis, and plenty of absorbent paper or cloth on which to dry them (see Fig 2.4).

Palettes

When using dyes and stains, it is important to decant the required amount into a palette and not use them straight from the container. The palette need not be elaborate. A plastic display tray from the supermarket, jam jar lids or small glass pots can all be used, and are just as effective as artist's ceramic palettes. However, bear in mind that spirit dyes can dissolve certain plastics, so always decant them into ceramic or glass palettes.

Finishing

There is an enormous number of commercially prepared wood finishes at present on the market, making the selection of the right one a minefield for the inexperienced woodturner and finisher. Although descriptions, analysis and merits of all the available products would fill a book in themselves, lathe-turned objects do have their own special requirements. This helps to narrow the field down enormously, and the selection becomes more manageable as a result (see Fig 2.5).

Finishes are applied to turned work after colouring, and sometimes to plain wood before grain filling. They include sanding sealer, French polish, oils, waxes and catalysed lacquers. Always remember that compatibility is the key to successful finishing; this becomes very much an issue when colouring your work, as there are some finishes which are not compatible with dyes and stains.

Fig 2.5
A selection of finishes and finish applicators: buffing brush, applicator brush, neutral wax, a carnauba or wax stick, sanding sealer, French polishes, Finishing oil and Danish oil.

To begin with, play safe and use the straightforward techniques and products recommended here, then add others as your experience grows and you feel confident to explore further.

There are two main types of finish which can be applied to coloured, turned work.

Decorative finish

The first I call a decorative finish, which uses a sealer followed by a polish – a spirit-based sanding sealer and a neutral, transparent wax give very good results. You can also use a pale French polish as the sealer, with a neutral wax polish on top. For the majority of decorative items, either of these combinations will give a satisfactory result.

Domestic finish

This is a waterproof, stain-resistant finish, achieved by using any of the hard-setting, tung oil based products, and is applied with a brush or soft paper. You can choose from pure tung oil, Danish oil or Finishing oil. The first two of these I find rather slow drying, and tending to give a slightly yellow tinge to the finished work. Finishing oil on the other hand is light, penetrating, quick drying and, being much clearer, does not impose any particular tone on the wood.

This is the kind of finish you might consider for bowls and other items to be used with food. You can also choose to use sunflower oil or any other light vegetable oil, but these will require replacing every time the item is used as they are not waterproof and will wash off the surface. Because of this they are not suitable for use over dyed surfaces.

Successful polishing

I use a pair of brushes to polish work where I have used wax as the final finishing coat; one to apply the polish to the revolving or stationary work, the other to buff up the rotating polished wood. Final buffing is then carried out with a cloth in the normal way.

Using brushes allows me to apply the polish *into* the grain rather than over it, with the result that the number of light-reflective surfaces being polished is greatly increased, and improves the depth and quality of the shine.

I have also found that a round drill brush is extremely useful for polishing off. Instead of the work rotating and the polishing brush being held against it, fix the drill brush into a Jacobs chuck and mount it in the lathe. Then hold the work up to the rotating brush. This is extremely effective for polishing the undersides of coloured bowls and platters which can sometimes be difficult to finish while on the lathe.

Quick-reference guide to a better polished finish

Unfilled open-grain wood	Brush on and brush off
Filled open-grain	Cloth on, cloth off
Close-grain wood	Cloth on, brush off, finish with soft cloth

Don't be tempted to burnish coloured wood with wood shavings as they can scratch the surface and even transfer spilt dye colours on to the work.

Types of finish

French polish

French polish is a solution of shellac and alcohol (either methylated spirit and/or ethanol). The substance is flammable and toxic, so safe storage and careful handling are essential. One or two coats can be used, rubbing down the dry first coat with steel wool before applying the second.

A full-blown French polish finish can be achieved over colour in the same way as it can on natural wood. This requires successive coats of polish used to fill the grain, rubbing down ('cutting back') between coats with fine steel wool, and keeping the surface clean using a tack cloth. Once the polish has satisfactorily filled the grain, make a cloth pad (traditionally known as a rubber), and apply the finishing coats of polish while the work is stationary, finally burnishing the revolving work using burnishing cream.

This method will give a highly glazed finish on coloured turned work, but can also darken the colour which has been used. Because of this I tend to restrict my use of French polish to a sealer prior to wax polishing.

White polish

This is made using bleached shellac flakes, and is a good sealer for bleached or white-stained pieces.

Sanding sealer

Spirit-based sanding sealer provides a highly successful finish over dyes and stains. It forms a barrier between the coloured wood and the wax polished surface. Sanding sealer is not waterproof or stain-resistant, and should only be used with wax polish as a decorative finish on pieces which will not be subjected to a great deal of handling. It can be applied by brush to small areas or with a pad of soft paper on larger areas, allowing you to cover as much of the work as possible before the sealer becomes tacky.

On large areas of close-grained wood, such as a sycamore platter, the absorption rates over the face of the timber will be extremely variable due to the contrasting grain formation. As with dyes, the absorption of sealer will be much greater on end grain than on side grain. It is therefore necessary to apply a very thin initial coat, and follow this with a normal second coat. If you still find the results unsatisfactory, try an oiled and polished finish as an alternative.

Lacquers

Do not use cellulose or melamine sealers or lacquers over dyes and stains unless you intend to spray them on. This is because the cellulose base is likely to pull up the dye and drag it, forming a blotchy effect. When sprayed on it is possible to get a good finish, as the cellulose simply lies on top of the dye and will not be mixed with it.

Precatalysed lacquers are the most appropriate type of lacquer for the woodturner, and provide a useful coating for small items which require a hard wearing finish such as door knobs and light pulls. However, the lacquer will need to be thinned down a little and then sprayed on, or used as a dip, since brushing will again bleed the dye. Such lacquers are available in satin, matt or gloss finishes.

Oils

There are several proprietary makes of oil available for use over dyes and stains. Pure tung oil is non-toxic and dries to a stainproof, heatproof, water-resistant finish. Due to its viscosity, it can be a little tricky to apply, and it takes at least 24 hours' drying time between each coat.

Tung is also the basis for other oil finishes such as Danish oil and Finishing oil. These contain thinners and dryers to improve handling and drying times.

In all cases, apply several light coats after an initially generous application to allow for absorption by the wood. The lighter the oil, of course, the more readily the wood will absorb it. Leave the first coat to soak in for about 15 minutes before wiping away any excess. Allow to dry thoroughly, cut back with fine steel wool, and proceed with the next coat. Be careful not to handle the work until it is fully dry each time!

Applied with care, oil finishes provide a beautiful, waterproof and stainproof finish which can be buffed to a sheen with a soft cloth. The level of shine can be increased by applying a coat of neutral wax polish and then buffing.

You can mix tung oil based products with spirit dyes, enabling you to dye and finish a piece at the same time. However, you will still need to apply at least three coats of the mixture for an effective, waterproof finish. For decorative purposes, one or two coats of oil and a coat of wax polish will suffice.

Sunflower and other vegetable oils are not recommended because they do not provide a permanent finish, are not water- or stainproof, and can go rancid if not freshly applied on a regular basis after the item has been washed.

Waxes

There are several makes of wax polish available, and all can be applied to stationary work using a brush, or with a safety cloth. (I use a short-haired 1in (25mm) paintbrush.)

Wax polishes are generally labelled as clear or neutral. I prefer a transparent finish over colour (you will find such waxes look white in the tin). Polish that has any colour in it will affect the colour of the dye used on the piece, usually having a darkening effect.

A carnauba block can be used on revolving spindle or end grain turning to give a high-class hard gloss finish. Carnauba is made from an extract from Brazilian palm trees and in its raw form is very hard and brittle. To make it suitable for use by the woodturner it is mixed with other waxes (frequently beeswax), and is sometimes referred to as a wax stick. The beeswax acts as a carrier and filler, allowing the carnauba to spread over the surface. You will find that different makes of wax stick will vary in use depending on the proportion of carnauba to beeswax. Try one or two to find the combination you prefer.

A single pass along revolving spindle work with a wax stick is usually enough. Begin at one end and, with safety cloth or paper, move evenly along the work, applying just sufficient pressure to create enough heat to melt the wax. You will see a ring of soft wax preceding your pass as it melts. Do not make a reverse pass.

If some rings of wax remain, it usually means there is too much on the wood, or that the wax has not melted evenly. Simply make another pass in the same direction, right to the end of the piece.

Do not use carnauba on faceplate work; the great variation between peripheral and central speeds of bowls and platters, along with the increased likelihood of vibration, makes it extremely hard to obtain an even spread of the wax.

Varnish stains

These are a colour and a finish all in one, and can be either spirit-based or water-based. The latter are usually non-toxic.

Varnish stains give a robust and durable finish, and as such I do not favour them for use on decorative and artistic turning. However, they are especially suitable as a finish for toys and household items, and are available in a good range of colours. For best results attempt to work in a dust-free atmosphere, and allow a drying and hardening time of three or four hours.

Coloured varnishes can be either brushed or sprayed on to the work. Two coats usually provide a good quality and hard wearing finish. Don't be tempted to increase the density of colour with too many coats, as one of the advantages of this type of finish is that you will still be able to see the grain through it.

These varnishes are available in a wide range of spectrum colours, as well as in pastel shades and wood colours. All the colours are pigments in suspension, and are not therefore absorbed by the wood, but are a surface covering only.

Overview

For the best results from all products, be they dyes, stains, sealers or finishes, always allow plenty of time for natural drying. As you have seen, drying times for different products vary considerably, and can even vary for the same product depending on the conditions under which drying takes place. Water-based dyes, for example, are dependent on water evaporation time, and this in turn will be influenced by the climate and ambient temperature. Drying and setting times are always shown on individual products, and it is always best to follow the manufacturer's recommendations.

Tools and materials for obtaining special effects

Fig 2.6
A selection of equipment for use in achieving special effects: gold and silver markers, permanent marker pen, liming wax, various fontenay bases, gilt varnish, wood bleach, gold size, metal transfer leaves, gilt cream, car spray paint, and patinating wax.

Later in this book I shall be explaining how to apply liming wax, which is a white grain filler, and patinating wax, which is a black grain filler. Both are available in ready to use form.

A gilded effect can set off any piece in a most spectacular way, and is easily achieved using proprietary gilt varnishes and gilt creams. Both are available in a range of colours which include bronze, gold, silver and copper. Another slightly more complicated method involves the use of fine metal transfer leaves which are adhered with gold size. These are available in gold, silver and copper.

Gilt creams and varnishes are best applied over a base coat of either fontenay or ready-made gesso (bole). As a general rule, red fontenay or gesso is used under the gold-colour gilts, and black fontenay or gesso under the silver colours, each of which provides a good undertone. However, yellow and white gesso and fontenay are also available.

Gold marker pens or paint pens are useful for very fine work, and gilt filler sticks can be used for filling natural blemishes or designer textures (see Fig 2.6).

Airbrushes

Once you have mastered the basic techniques of colouring, and have become familiar with a range of special effects, you may wish to try achieving coloured finishes with an airbrush. There are three types of airbrush from which to choose.

Single action

This has an air control button on top of a hand piece which is depressed to activate the air and paint supply. The paint-to-air ratio cannot be adjusted, and the delivery pattern of the spray cannot be altered, except by altering the distance of the nozzle from the work.

Double action

This allows the amount of paint released in a constant air stream to be varied. It can be fed in gradually, suddenly tailed away, or stopped immediately.

Independent double action

This gives the user the greatest control over the brush, allowing for infinite variation of delivery, from intense line work to a wide-angle mist (see Fig 2.7). A top mounted lever can control the air supply when depressed and the paint supply when pulled back.

There are several models from which to choose, covering a wide price range. It is a good idea to look at and test the feel of different hand pieces to find one that is comfortable to use before making your selection from those models which have the mechanical features that you require.

It is useful to have extra airbrush jars to hold different dyes, which can then be readily used in succession as they are easily unscrewed from the holder and replaced.

Airbrushes are fun to use, but before rushing out to buy one, do remember that you will also need a compressor. As with the airbrush, the more sophisticated the compressor the more expensive it will be. Storage and piston compressors are both suitable, but an automatic compressor is probably the best. It will cut in

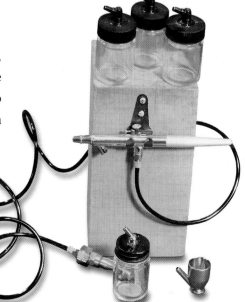

Fig 2.7
Independent double action airbrush.

and out automatically, and so provide a constant supply of compressed air.

Stencils

Stencilling can be an alternative to freehand designs. I find the use of a self-adhesive masking film the most effective, using a scalpel and board to achieve a clear-cut design with tidy edges. This same self-adhesive film can be used as a resist to leave an uncoloured area of wood when airbrushing dye.

Turntables

Of course there are occasions when it pays to take a colour project into your home, especially if you are dyeing a complex pattern or design. It is helpful to sit down and work in comfort at a table, especially if the piece needs to be flat, or is large enough to require a considerable amount of time spent on it. In these circumstances I have found a turntable an enormous help. I use a potter's turntable approximately 8in (203mm) in diameter and 6in (152mm) high. It is stable but turns very smoothly. Alternatively, try using a cake icing turntable, or making your own using a lazy susan ball-bearing race (see Fig 2.8).

Fig 2.8
A potter's turntable or a cake icing turntable are useful items, allowing you to revolve your work easily.

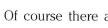

Lathes

A book on colouring techniques is not an appropriate place for a lengthy consideration of the relative merits of different lathes and associated equipment. But for those who have not previously tried it, for spindle turning, I would strongly recommend the use of a ring centre drive together with a revolving centre in the tailstock (see Fig 2.9).

The use of the ring centre as a friction drive was piloted by my husband about 17 years ago and, following his lead and enthusiasm for it, many turners tried it and now find it indispensable. It has an adjustable centre pin which is valuable when using a variety of hard and soft woods. The pin can also be removed and the drive used in the tailstock for long hole boring. I find it has great advantages over other drives especially when doing batch work between centres.

There are several advantages to this type of drive. First, the safety aspect. Should the turner inadvertently have a 'dig in' then the work will stop immediately while the ring centre continues to revolve harmlessly in the work, causing no damage to turner or wood.

Second, the work can quickly and deftly be turned end for end and will relocate accurately. This is not only useful when facing off the ends but provides a third advantage in that it gives you the facility to perform reverse sanding between centres!

Fourth, it allows you to stop the work to check it for finishing quality without switching off the lathe. Simply take the pressure off the tailstock, which allows the work to stop spinning. Inspect it, and then tighten up the tailstock to continue turning. Another advantage is the mark made in the wood by the drive. Far from being ugly and requiring to be removed before the finished piece of work can be handed to its new owner, the pin and ring mark is the same as that frequently added to the work by many aspiring turners for decorative effect, and preferable by far to the mark made by a four prong drive (see Fig 2.10).

Above **Fig 2.9**
A ring centre drive.

Below **Fig 2.10**
Marks made on the work by a ring centre drive (left) and a four prong drive (right).

CHAPTER 3

Timber

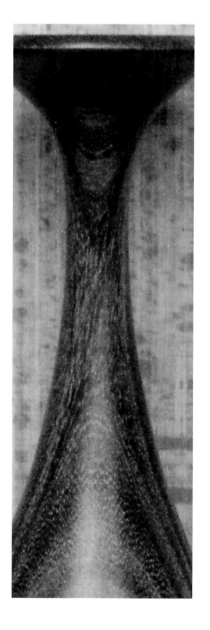

I am lucky enough to drive each day through a beautiful tree-lined avenue into a parkland estate, where I have my workshop and showroom in what was an old estate carpenter's shop. When visitors to this West Country wildlife park come into the workshop, they invariably ask me what sort of wood I am using and which are the best woods for turning. I always reply that it is possible to turn virtually any timber. It is just that some woods are more satisfying to turn than others, and some may be more suitable for a particular job. It is just the same with colouring.

Any wood can be coloured by dyeing or staining, but different timbers respond in a variety of ways, some with more pleasing results than others. The success of the colouring is dependent on the density of the timber, its grain formation and the extent of the effect of the timber's own colour beneath the dye.

Grain and the colourist

If you already turn wood, you will know that it is an extremely versatile medium with which to work. When colouring turned work, it is important that you take into consideration its complex cellular structure, which causes it to absorb moisture at different rates and to different depths over its surface. Because end grain is capable of absorbing far more moisture than side grain, colour definition will be greater on end grain, while side grain will appear much lighter with the same coverage of dye. This phenomenon is further accentuated with turned work, which tends to display a surface of varying amounts of end and side grain side by side.

Fig 3.1 shows two areas of side grain in a turned vase: on the body where the circumference is greatest, and on the narrowest part of the neck (a). The remaining profile displays varying degrees of end grain (b), and the whole piece is therefore subject to varying rates of dye absorption.

Both the exterior and the interior of a bowl turned from a plank of wood will display two areas of side grain and two of end grain (see Fig 3.2). The difference in the

Below **Fig 3.1**
Areas of side grain (a), and end grain (b) on a turned vase.

Bottom **Fig 3.2**
A bowl turned from a plank of wood, showing areas of side and grain (a) and end grain (b).

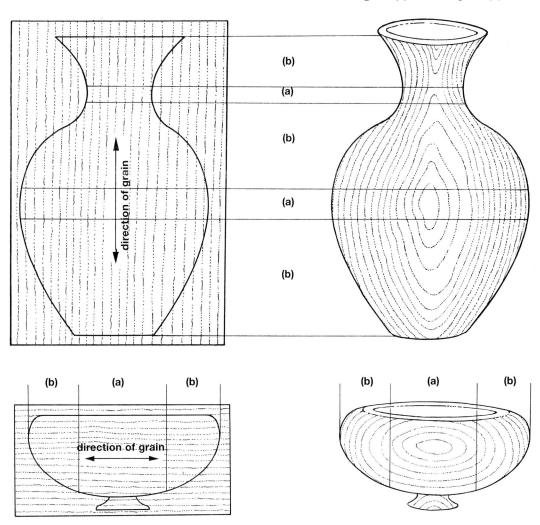

ability of the various areas to absorb equal amounts of dye is clear and results in uneven colouring. For some colourists this can be a major source of irritation, but there are ways of turning the situation to your advantage, by making the colour variation look intentional (refer to Fig 9.11, on page 101).

Obtaining timber

However, the question I am most frequently asked is 'where do you get your wood?' Newcomers to woodturning are not always armed with the fertile imagination needed to acquire the raw materials on a limited budget!

Your local timber merchant is a good place to start. Woodworking magazines also carry adverts from specialist timber stockists. These two sources are convenient but costly. It also takes patience when selecting wood from a timber store, to check for splits, cracks, warping, drying checks, and so on. Even with the greatest care it is impossible to guarantee the quality, but it does pay to look carefully especially as timber is so expensive.

However, the turner does not need to be as choosy as the cabinetmaker, and if the wood is not good enough for turning there is always the alternative of using it to keep warm – wood need never be wasted!

There are alternative sources of timber. Recycling is one. This means keeping an eye open for signs of house renovation, shop refitting or hotel refurbishment. In all cases there is sure to be old timber available for the asking.

When friends know you turn, you'll be surprised how many trees are offered to you. These may be either sick, storm damaged or overgrown trees, and are often fruit woods or laurel. You may need to hire, beg or borrow lifting gear, chainsaws and suitable transport if you are offered a very large section of tree, or even a whole tree. In such cases it pays to share your spoil with a fellow turner or woodworker, who either has access to such equipment or is willing to share the cost of equipment hire.

You will then need to either turn the whole lot while it is green or store it until you have reached old age while it seasons – the general rule is one year per 1in (25mm) thickness for seasoning. Alternatively, you may decide to invest in a dehumidifier and kiln-dry the timber. This would give you dry wood in about three months.

When you look about, you will be amazed at the number of things we use and see on a daily basis that are made from wood, and in due course are discarded for burning or recycling.

Choosing a suitable wood

Before starting on a specific job or project, stop to consider all the factors which need to be taken into account when choosing a suitable wood. These include the type of project, the intended design, the colour and type of dye you will use, any special effects you have planned, and the intended finish. Then list the possible timbers from which your choice might be made, taking into account those which are reasonably available. Table 3.1 (on page 36) is designed to provide you with some initial guidelines on suitable woods for different pieces.

Whichever wood you choose, you may end up having to adjust your design a little due to the fact that the colour you have chosen does not look quite the way you expected it to when applied to the wood. This is inevitable on occasion, but a careful choice of wood in relation to your project will prevent it happening too often.

Let us look at an example. Say you wanted to turn and colour a small stool for children, which needs to have a hardwearing finish but is at the same time attractive to look at. You decide on a simple colouring material: a blue acrylic water-based stain (Chapter 8 shows you how to construct and colour a similar project in detail), and on liming as your special effect (see Fig 3.3). The stool will need to be water-proof and stainproof, so a tung oil based product is chosen

Table 3.1 Projects, with suitable timbers

Project	Type of dye	Special effect	Suitable woods
Salad bowl	Water-based dye	Blended dye on exterior	Ash Sycamore Beech
Candleholder	Water-based dye	Limed	Ash Oak Chestnut
Large platter	Spirit dye	Patterned rim	Sycamore Lime Maple
Pedestal bowl	Water-based dye	Oiled inside, polished outside	**Bowl**: holly; apple; maple **Pedestal**: ash; chestnut
Hollow form	Acrylic water-based stain	Ebonised	Mahogany Sycamore
Decorative vase	Water-based dye	Gilt grain filler	Ash Iroko Chestnut

Fig 3.3
Ash is an ideal timber for a project
such as this low stool, which has
been coloured and limed.

as the best finish. You have elm, oak, beech and ash
available; which is the best timber to choose?

Elm is becoming increasingly rare and has a good
depth of natural colour, over which it is difficult to lay a
pastel colour satisfactorily. You could go for the oak; it
has an open grain ideal for liming, but the tannin in the
wood can tend to alter the applied colour (in this case it
would be likely to bring out green tones in the blue
stain). Beech would provide a good base colour on
which to apply the acrylic stain, but does not have an
open grain, making it unsuitable for liming.

Ash is the best choice here; it responds accurately to
colour, has a flowing and open grain ideal for liming, and
you can normally find a piece that is uniformly pale in
colour to provide an even-toned base for colouring.

Of course, there may well be natural stains and blemishes in the timber and variations of natural colour (olive ash is a good example of this), as well as those markings caused by disease, which are frequently seen in spalted beech (see Fig 3.4). They must all be taken into consideration, since, when using dyes, they will not be hidden. Dye is transparent, allowing you to see the grain of the wood and any natural markings. For me this is one of the delights of using dye. Stains are slightly more opaque, but still allow the grain to be seen.

The quality of timber may vary from tree to tree in the same species, serving as a reminder that wood is a natural material which does not lend itself to uniformity. An inferior quality wood can affect the finish of your

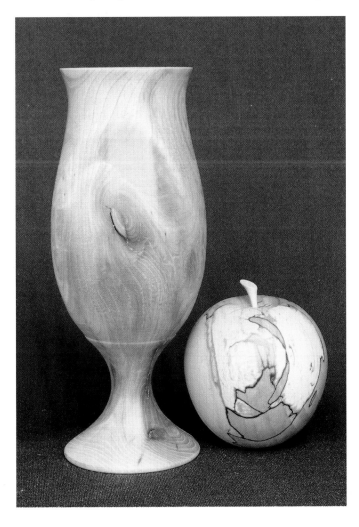

Fig 3.4
Two pieces turned in olive ash (left) and spalted beech (right). Highly figured timbers may be regarded as unsuitable for colouring.

work, notably when the fibres are softening. This may occur sporadically, even in a single board or log. Sometimes you may not be aware of the poor quality while turning and colouring, but it will become apparent when you try to get a decent finish at the polishing stage. You may find that the timber is so absorbent that an even shine is extremely difficult to obtain.

Each variety of timber has its own individual quirks and it takes time and experience in handling them to become really familiar with the different species and the remarkable natural colours and figuration of many timbers. Those which already have an intense and rich colour of their own are not, in my view, suitable for dyeing or staining since the addition of unnatural colour distracts from rather than enhances the natural wood.

Imported timbers such as partridge, bubinga, rosewood, and padauk display their own strong bright colours. Zebrano and wenge are among the two-tone crew, very dramatic and stagey and very striking, especially in the plainer company of oak, elm, beech, ash and pine (see Fig 3.5).

As a general rule, the hotter and drier the country, the darker and denser the wood. These colourful and exotic woods can create great contrast alongside the more reserved appeal of our indigenous timbers, but at what cost, not only

Fig 3.5
A selection of vases turned from imported timbers, showing the strength of natural colour in some woods. Left to right: zebrano, wenge, partridge, bubinga, rosewood and padauk.

to the pocket, but also to the world? We can assist both aspects by colouring the more plentiful and faster growing timbers in preference to turning the depleted exotic hardwoods. The naturally pale colour of temperate woods provides a great variety of first class timber for the colourist.

We are almost spoiled for choice when looking at home grown, close-grained woods. Apart from fruit and nut trees, we can also add London plane (known when harvested as lacewood), sycamore, hornbeam, birch, holly and maple, all of which display a light coloured surface, although an occasional highly figurative sample may come your way and will need to be treated sympathetically when colouring (see Fig 3.6).

These close-grained timbers are delightful as a medium on which to paint pictures or patterns with dye or stain, as they absorb the dyes readily and evenly. Sycamore and maple are also ideal for ebonising and stencilling.

Good quality pine can be turned and coloured satisfactorily, but attention to the finish of the prepared piece is essential, and I find acrylic stains give better results than dyes. But it pays to try both, as results are subject to personal preference.

For a greater selection of open-grained varieties, include sweet chestnut and acacia among our better known home-grown varieties of oak and ash. Of the imported woods available, European oak and American white oak are both good quality open-grained timbers for colouring. Red oak is very coarse and doesn't finish particularly well, but is cheaper and therefore useful for practising on. Brown oak is of good quality, but the fungal attack which causes the brown discoloration does such a good job that it displays too much of its own colour to be useful for spectrum colouring.

I have been delighted with the effects I have achieved on other disregarded woods, such as the poorer quality hardwoods like lauan and meranti. Iroko too, is most effective when coloured, although a dreadful timber to turn as the dust is extremely toxic. Should you decide to

Fig 3.6
An example of a highly figured piece of lacewood (London plane) which would need to be treated sympathetically with yellow dye to further highlight the markings.

experiment with this timber, be sure to wear a respirator when turning (see Chapter 4).

Lauan illustrates more graphically than most other readily available timbers the ability of wood to be turned from something of little artistic value into a piece of considerable interest. The timber has little appeal; the colour is uniform, and the grain non-existent except that it has a consistent open fleck. It has a very low density, giving little handling appeal, and is so soft that it disappears at the sight of abrasives. This, of course, makes lauan easy to turn and, when treated to some colour and grain filler, it can be totally transformed and in appearance joins the higher ranks of naturally superior timbers (see Figs 3.7 and 3.8). The same applies to iroko and meranti. Try turning and colouring these woods, and you will see what I mean!

An alternative to selecting a timber suitable for the job is to turn a variety of articles from whatever timber is available and then treat them individually. However, the quickest way of gaining experience in colouring and decorating timbers is to make a number of similar articles using the same wood. Turn several items

Fig 3.7
The insignificant composition of lauan wood is transformed with dyes, liming wax and copper gilt varnish.

Fig 3.8
Lauan vases, coloured and limed.

between centres, such as stool legs or candleholders, and several others on the faceplate, such as shallow dishes or platters. If you are afraid of spoiling your work with your first attempts at colouring, turn several cylinders and practise colouring techniques on these. As you grow more confident, turn them into specific shapes and colour them again.

As you progress, keep a note of the variety of timber, the type and colour of dye used, the drying times you have allowed, the type of finish, the number of applications, and so on. Most importantly, note down a comment on the success of the piece. You will find this will help you to get to know your timbers, dyes and techniques, and to develop your own individual style.

Be sure your timber is dry before turning and colouring; 10% moisture is a mean average to work to. It is worth investing in a moisture meter if you intend making a lot of bowls, dishes and platters, as it is on these forms that shrinkage and warping becomes most noticeable and can cause great disappointment (see Fig 3.9). A dry, well insulated timber store is a tremendous asset. It will limit the variation in temperature to which turned wood is subjected in its travels from damp woodstore as a blank, to the workshop to be turned and eventually to a centrally heated home. No wonder many pieces split or warp. Try to minimise these temperature variations by making sure that your own woodstore (be it custom-built, the garage, spare bedroom or workshop) is as dry as possible. Bring the wood into the warmer workshop some time before using it, and test its moisture content before turning. When the piece has been turned and coloured, advise the recipient not to take it straight into a very hot room but to help it acclimatise gradually by first putting it in a cooler part of the house. It will then not react badly to the central heating at a later date.

Wood is a versatile and resilient material, able to withstand the physical stress of the high seas and static loaded stress in buildings. It can be made waterproof and is mostly non-toxic, so is suitable for use with food. Much of it is visually appealing in character and extremely tactile. Above all, and especially for those of us who work with wood, the natural or acquired colour, particularly of old wood, and the patina gained over time from accidental or intentional use of caring hands, are a source of deep pleasure. However, it is surely the time for a renaissance in the use of spectrum colours on small turnery!

Fig 3.9
A moisture meter.

CHAPTER 4

Health and safety

I cannot emphasise too strongly that the observation of safety measures in the workshop is of paramount importance. This chapter is intended to provide sufficient information to ensure that the home workshop user works in an enjoyable yet safe environment.

When turning wood, and during the final preparation of a piece before colouring, always wear a face shield and a nose/mouth dust respirator (see Fig 4.1). These should be regarded as the minimum protection. Even though you may achieve a brilliant tool finish, there will always be a small amount of sanding necessary before the work is ready to be coloured.

It is imperative to protect the face – particularly the eyes – from even the remotest possibility of damage by wood dust or a piece of flying wood. Never think it won't happen to you. It just might.

Powered respirators

If at all possible, wear a battery-powered respirator when turning and sanding (see Fig 4.2). Regard the cost of acquiring one as a health insurance policy, as it is the very fine wood dust particles, created by fine abrasives, that are the most damaging when inhaled. The dust from some woods is notably more toxic and irritating to the bronchial system than others. Watch out for mahoganies and iroko, both of which are good for colouring, but

Fig 4.1
Face shield and a nose/mouth dust respirator.

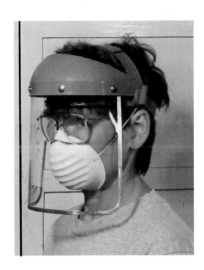

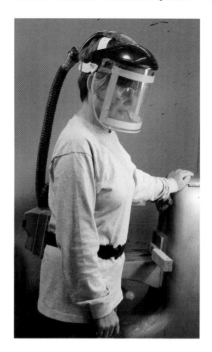

Fig 4.2
A powered respirator.

Fig 4.3
You can see how much dust accumulates in the filter of a powered respirator, and consequently how important it is to protect yourself from inhaling such dust.

whose dust can be very harmful if inhaled.

It is well known that many professional woodturners who, in the past, were unaware of the hazards of wood dust, have since become susceptible to dusts which previously did not affect them. The problem is that once damage to the system has been caused, it cannot be reversed. Regard turning without a respirator as being equally, if not more dangerous, than driving without a seat belt. It is just not worth the risk. I rely heavily on my powered respirator to protect my face and lungs, and know it to be extremely effective simply by looking at the amount of dust which accumulates in the filter (see Fig 4.3).

Although the visor of a respirator is essential for protecting your face against flying particles of wood, dust and splashes of harmful substances, it is equally important to be able to see properly through it! As wiping accumulated dust and muck from the visor can scratch it (as can contact with the bench), visors can quickly become so dirty that they represent a safety hazard due to impaired vision.

The answer, I have found, is to use transparent tear-off strips on the visor, which will protect it, and can be removed and replaced when they become dirty (see Fig 4.4). Always remember that it is vital that you are able to see the cutting edges of your tools and the worksurface clearly and in detail at all times.

To care for my powered respirator and consequently help to prolong its life, I always hang it up when not in use, ensuring that the air tube is not kinked (see Fig 4.5). This also allows me to plug it into the battery charger with ease whenever necessary.

Nose and mouth cartridge respirator

There are substances and finishes which, although good for the wood, can be damaging to the user, and against which powered respirators are not a protection. Always take great care when handling toxic products and avoid breathing the vapours or the mists when spraying such things as cellulose, paint, lacquers, spirit-based products and stains. Always have adequate ventilation in the workshop and if possible spray your work outside. Always remember that no matter how efficient your powered respirator may be, it cannot prevent you from breathing toxic fumes. Only a nose/mouth cartridge respirator offers such protection. This unit fits comfortably over the nose and mouth and, together with a pair of goggles, gives complete protection. Some cartridges will filter out dust as well.

Metal dust

Metal dust particles are just as damaging to your respiratory system as wood dust. They are usually created when using fine steel wool as part of the final preparation of a piece for colouring, and during the colouring process itself.

It is always wise to use scissors to cut the required length of steel wool, rather than tearing it (see Fig 4.6). Try tearing off a usable length, either in a shaft of sunlight or beneath your work lamp. Then cut off a similar length in the same light. The amount of dust produced by tearing the material will be clear, graphically illustrating the hazard. Remember, what is breathed in is not breathed out again!

Dust extraction systems

If you have room in your workshop to accommodate a dust extraction unit, then do so. Such units, used in conjunction with respiration equipment, will help to significantly reduce the risk of harmful dust inhalation.

Protective clothing

Try to wear protective clothing which is plain or zip fronted and has elasticated cuffs. These reduce the chances of

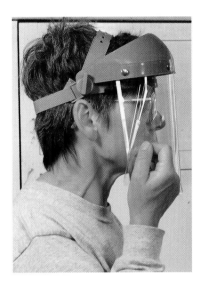

Fig 4.4
A transparent tear-off strip applied to the visor, which can easily be removed and disposed of when it becomes dirty.

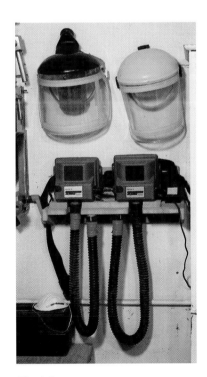

Fig 4.5
Hang up your respirator when not in use, ensuring that the hose is not kinked. This is also the time to recharge the batteries.

Fig 4.6
Cutting steel wool to length rather than tearing it significantly reduces the amount of metal dust you introduce into the air.

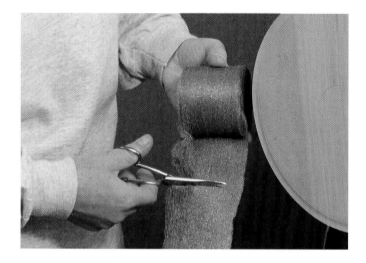

sleeves catching in machinery or trailing in liquids, and also protect your arms from irritating wood dust and the possibly harmful chemicals or toxic components of finishing products. When colouring, they also avoid the problem of trailing cuffs dragging one colour across another or on to uncoloured wood where it is not wanted.

When you have finished a job, remember to remove any dirty clothing before going indoors, perhaps to stand by an open fire – your garments may have become impregnated with flammable substances – and always wash your hands before touching food to avoid accidentally ingesting anything poisonous.

Do not wear fine rubber gloves as protection from toxic substances or for turning wood on the lathe. Although these are ideal for keeping your hands clean when applying, say, black patinating wax (see Chapter 16), they can easily be whipped off if they come into contact with the revolving work, and they may be melted by toxic substances and sealers.

Using and storing products in the workshop

A well-organised workshop, with your materials arranged in an orderly way in cupboards or on shelves, all correctly labelled and kept well out of harm's way, makes a huge contribution to the health and safety of those who use it or visit it. This applies particularly to toxic substances (see Fig 4.7).

Toxic or non-toxic?

Many modern products, such as dyes, have now been developed which are non-toxic, making them far safer and easier to handle. However, always check the suitability of a product for the job in hand before purchasing. If your project is intended as a children's toy, or for serving food on, check for the British Standard Safety Number BS5665, which indicates the product has been tested by an authorised laboratory and found to be free from toxicity once the solutions have dried on the wood. Never interpret the lack of a hazard symbol as a sign of non-toxicity; always check with the shop or supplier before purchasing.

You will find it is often more economical to buy products in bulk, which leads to the need to safely decant them before use. Always ensure that the container into which you intend to decant a product is made of a suitable material; some products are quite capable of dissolving some plastics!

Guard against loss by evaporation from your smaller containers by using well-fitting lids, and ensure these are on tightly. Always label any new containers to remind you exactly what is in them – believe me, it is *very* easy to forget.

Do not return left over dyes to the containers from which they were decanted, as this can easily alter the colour and spoil the whole lot. The smallest amounts of another dye or any other substance in the decanted product can ruin the colour of the original supply.

Always read the labels before using products together to ensure compatibility between your chosen dye and finish. If both contain, or respond to, the same solvent, then the second application will dissolve the first and make an awful mess. I know – I've done it!

Fig 4.7
A well-ordered and secure storage area for your materials significantly increases your working efficiency and decreases the chances of accidents in the workshop.

Solvents

Be familiar with the contents of the products you buy, and always be aware of what a product's solvent is. This makes it much easier during and at the end of a work session to quickly clean out brushes or mop up spillages effectively.

If you have used cloths or paper roll for cleaning brushes with spirit, or that are soaked with other flammable liquids, don't leave them bundled up in the workshop where they could ignite spontaneously. Spread out any such cloths if they are to be re-used, and incinerate waste paper on a daily basis.

Safe storage and identification of substances

Always keep chemicals and flammable substances in a locked, preferably metal cupboard, well away from any heat source, well out of the reach of children. If substances lose their labels, you can decant them to aid in recognition by colour, viscosity and odour, but do not sniff them close-to. Hold the substance away from you and waft any fumes towards you while breathing very gently. If in doubt, always dispose of such unidentified substances safely. Never tip them directly into a water course; put them in well-stoppered containers and consult your local waste-disposal expert.

Visitors

A 'please knock' sign on your workshop door is a good idea. When your lathe is running or you have a radio on it can be difficult to hear someone coming in, and if you are startled by a sudden presence it could lead to an accident due to a lapse in your concentration. Try to educate regular visitors to knock, call out, or wait at a distance until you see them before they approach the lathe or workbench.

Smoking

Don't smoke in the workshop. Display a suitable 'no smoking' sign for the benefit of visitors who may not appreciate the fire risk. Don't be afraid to invite people to step outside for a few minutes if they wish to smoke. Provide a bucket of sand near the door for cigarettes to be easily and safely extinguished. Such a bucket also provides a useful means of extinguishing small fires, though you should always have a fire extinguisher in your workshop and keep it regularly maintained.

Heating

The best way to heat the workshop is with central heating pipes running from an adjacent building. If this is not possible, an oil filled radiator or purpose built sawdust burner both provide efficient closed heat sources. Do not ever be tempted to have an open fire in the workshop – if keeping warm becomes a problem, put on another layer of clothing, or wait until the weather becomes milder. Cold workshops are not much fun to work in, nor do they provide the right conditions for successful colouring.

Lighting

The quality of lighting in the workshop is extremely important, and is a subject which is sometimes not given the attention it deserves. From a safety point of view, it is very important to work in good light, especially when you are using sharp tools and machinery. Good light is also important to enable you to accurately observe technical details of your work, such as the fit of a box lid, or to assess the correct colour when colouring.

The best kind of light to work in is daylight similar to that of a bright but overcast day, giving even and consistent illumination. For the majority of us however, daylight must be supplemented with electric light, and it is worth experimenting with different types of electric light to see which suits you and your workshop best. You might choose strip lighting, daylight simulation bulbs, or a combination of the two. However, you will almost certainly need a spotlight, preferably the adjustable type, positioned directly over your work, so as to create shadows which will help you to determine the quality of the surface in terms of tool and sanding marks, especially when working on a long, undulating profile.

Safety when using the lathe

When you are giving your newly coloured piece of work its final polish, use a safety cloth in order to eliminate any risk of damage to yourself or the work (see page 17). You can also use ordinary soft absorbent paper which will give similar results and provide the same level of safety protection.

Should you decide to use a woven polishing rag, take great care. The same applies to the use of steel wool; this also runs the risk of getting caught on the work, and you can lessen the risk by tucking in the ends towards the middle, making a roll (see Fig 4.8). Alternatively, opt for commercially prepared steel wool rolls, which have no loose ends.

Finally, when mounting a new blank on a lathe, or remounting a prepared piece for colouring, always remember to check the lathe speed, and alter it if necessary, before switching on the motor. The larger the piece of wood, the slower the speed needs to be to ensure safe turning, colouring or finishing. Whether between centres, faceplate or end grain turning, excessive peripheral speed could easily create sufficient vibration to cause the wood to break loose from its mountings, with potentially dire consquences.

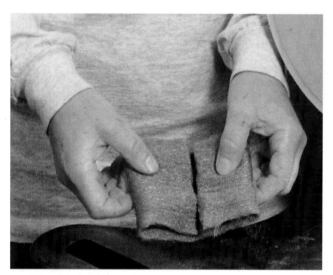

Fig 4.8
Tucking in the ends of steel wool towards the middle will reduce the risk of it getting caught on the work.

CHAPTER 5

Preparations for colouring

Environment

The best results from colouring wood are obtained if the work is done in a warm, dry workspace in a dust free environment. Dust is very mischievous; it can affect colour, as well as the quality of the finish, so I suggest preparing several items for colouring at the same time. Clean up the workspace after turning and sanding operations are complete and allow the dust to settle before embarking on dyeing or staining. For the woodturner/colourist, the height of luxury would be to have a separate room in which to colour finished pieces away from the place of making. However, this would require two lathes; one on which to turn and another on which to remount the work for colouring and finishing. So, for most of us, the only solution is to clean up the workshop!

Drying times

Each product has its own drying time, and to obtain the best results it is absolutely essential to allow them to dry naturally and thoroughly. This applies to any liquid product mentioned in this book. There is a risk of compromising the efficiency of the product and the finish achieved if drying times are not observed.

The drying time for a water-based dye, for example, is entirely dependent upon the speed of evaporation of the

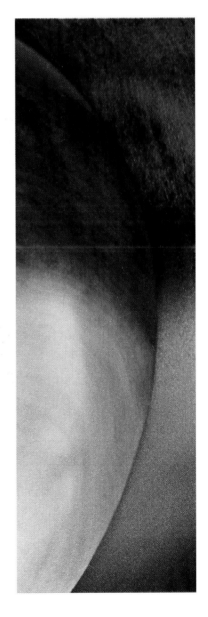

water from the wood. Hence, a warm ambient temperature will contribute dramatically to the speed of drying.

End grain

Any article which is to be coloured should be prepared with the same amount of care as it would receive for normal finishing, paying particular attention to finishing cuts and removing any sign of torn grain or concentric sanding marks. Far from the dye covering sanding marks or blemishes, it will in fact accentuate them, especially on end grain, due to the fact that it has a greater rate of absorption than side grain, and will therefore show a greater depth of colour (see Fig 5.1).

Fig 5.1
The poor surface finish on the right shows how dye accentuates torn grain and concentric sanding marks. Careful preparation of the wood will avoid this, resulting in the smooth finish you can see on the left of the cylinder.

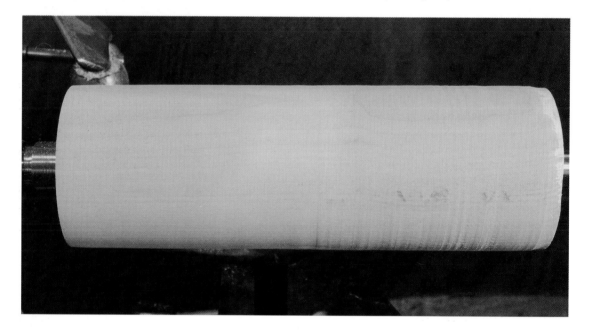

The fibres of side grain on a cylinder or plank of wood absorb a moderate amount of dye but, because the surface is even, the absorption rate is fairly even, giving an evenly coloured effect. However, once curves are added to the profile, the absorbency rate immediately changes. As all curved surfaces display varying degrees of end grain, there will be varying rates of absorption of dye (refer to Figs 3.1 and 3.2 on page 33). This will result in varying colour intensities over the piece, though not necessarily particularly obvious or detrimental to the overall effect. It is, however, important to appreciate this phenomenon so that you adjust the pressure used with steel wool when rubbing down over the varying contours between coats of dye or sealer and polish.

Final sanding

After making the finishing tool cuts on a piece, work through the increasingly finer grit abrasives, say from 120 through to 320, making sure that the grit you are using is doing its work efficiently and effectively (see Fig 5.2). Don't move on to a finer grit until the sanding marks of the

Fig 5.2
Use progressively finer abrasives to achieve a fine finish. Always make sure the grit you are using is not worn.

previous one have been removed and, most importantly, don't expect a worn out 240 to do the job of a 320 grit. The type of abrasion is completely different and can be rather akin to using blunt tools. A worn out grit will create heat and also flatten the fibres of the wood, in effect polishing a less than perfect finish instead of having the clean cutting effect of a new, finer grit abrasive.

The versatility of fabric-backed abrasive means that it is particularly useful in dealing with curved items when sanding in Vs or other restricted areas. Should the edge of the fabric tend to collapse from lack of substance, simply hold a piece of card abrasive behind it for support.

You will also find it beneficial to stop the lathe in order to use the final abrasive *with* the grain as opposed to *across* the grain, which is what is happening the whole time the lathe is running. It is this attention to detail that helps to produce high quality work at the end of the day.

When sanding is complete, rub over the work with grade 0000 steel wool, and finish by wiping off with a tack cloth to ensure a really clean surface ready for colouring.

Grain raising

When applied to wood, water-based dyes will naturally raise the grain. To minimise this undesirable reaction, raise the grain first by wetting the surface of the work with a brush or damp sponge and clean water (see Fig 5.3). The wood fibres swell as they reach out for the moisture, and up comes the grain. Allow the work to dry, and then, with very fine abrasive (say 400 grit or, depending on the coarseness of the timber, grade 0000 steel wool) cut back the raised grain. Then wipe off with a tack cloth. Coarser-grained woods such as oak or chestnut will require a slightly stronger abrasive than close-grained woods like lime or apple.

Fig 5.3
Grain raising. Wet the surface with a brush or, as here, a damp sponge.

Even spirit dyes have a grain raising effect on wood, so for the best results, prepare all your work in the same way prior to colouring with any type of dye or other finish. If this procedure is not adopted, the ultimate finish will leave much to be desired. The smooth or silken feel of the finished piece depends enormously on the standard and quality of the preparation of the work prior to colouring (see Fig 5.4).

Now the wood is ready for dyeing. If you are using a water-based dye, you will find that the grain raising response of the wood will be minimal.

Fig 5.4
Fine abrasive, steel wool and a tack cloth, all used in the final preparation of the work after grain raising and before colouring.

Final preparations

Select the items you need for a particular project, and arrange them on a table or bench, so that you can easily pick up what you need. For most dyeing projects this list will include your choice of dye and a palette into which it can be decanted, a brush or sponge applicator for applying the dye, and two or three pots or jars for washing them in. You will also need a supply of clean water with which to wash brushes used for water-based dyes, and a bucket in which to discard brush rinsing water, unless you are fortunate enough to have a handy sink, or a drain and water tap. Alternatively, you may need white spirit and a suitable container in which to clean out brushes which have been used for spirit dyes.

For cutting back raised fibres or less than perfect surfaces between coats of dye or finishes, have ready some grade 0000 steel wool, some 400 grit abrasive, and a tack cloth. You will also need to have an appropriate finish to hand, such as sanding sealer and wax polish, or one of the oils suggested in Chapter 2, together with the necessary brushes, a safety cloth and some disposable soft paper.

If you have followed my suggestion and prepared several items for colouring at the same time, you may find that when they are remounted on the lathe, either on a chuck or between centres, they do not run quite true. This may be because the centres have been slightly moved, or because of the uneven shrinkage of spigots which are held in a chuck. It could also be the result of straightforward warping or distortion, such as frequently happens after turning, especially with larger bowls or platters. The more wood that is removed and the thinner the vessel wall, the more likely is the piece to distort. However, although a piece may be out of true when remounted, this need not give cause for great concern as you will not need to make any further tool cuts, and the flexibility of brushes and cloths will overcome the slight eccentricity when applying polishes and cutting back between applications with steel wool.

I had not imagined anyone trying to apply dye to revolving spindle work, until a young husband and wife approached me as I was demonstrating at one of the national woodturning shows. The wife asked if I might be able to give her husband some advice about colouring wood. He had apparently tried it many times with less than satisfactory degrees of success, each time returning to the house from his workshop with severely dye-splattered overalls and a report that the workshop wall was becoming increasingly colourful. His face was a picture of amazed embarrassment as I gave him the solution to his problem – dye is applied while the work is stationary (see Fig 5.5). If dye is applied to revolving spindlework, you will suffer the same serious attack of dye splatter! When you are experienced and confident with dye and stain applications, then centrifuging faceplate work can be added to your list of techniques

Fig 5.5
Dye is always applied when the work is stationary, unless you are considering the centrifuging technique (see Chapter 12).

(see Chapter 12), but, for all other purposes, apply dye with the lathe switched off. Although dyes, sealers, oils and grain fillers are applied while the work is stationary, the lathe is turned on for fine abrading, taking off excesses after grain filling, and when polishing. I would recommend reducing the lathe speed when carrying out these processes during colouring.

CHAPTER 6

Colour and its applications

Colour theory

For the purposes of colouring turned work, it is not necessary to have any specialist knowledge about the make-up of dyes and pigments, or to know all the complexities of colour mixing. However, a little knowledge of colour theory will give you more confidence, and consequently lots more fun and potential for positive creativity.

The colours of the spectrum are the colours of the rainbow, with which most of us are familiar. These colours are not clearly defined, but blend from one to the next. They always maintain the same order: red, orange, yellow, green, blue, indigo, and violet (see Fig 6.1).

On closer examination you will see that each colour between the spectrum colours can be obtained by mixing the colours on either side of it. By adding purple to the list, which would be made by mixing red and violet, we could

Fig 6.1
The colour spectrum.

create a continuous line of colour blending.

The white light we get from the sun contains all the colours of the rainbow, so when natural light is available, all objects reflect a part of that light. A white object reflects virtually all the white light containing all the rainbow colours, and so appears white. A black object absorbs virtually all white light and, because hardly any is reflected, will appear black. Because surfaces of objects reflect or absorb light in varying degrees, we see varying shades of particular colours, and this goes for shades of black and white as well.

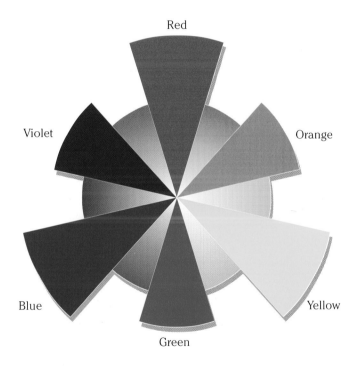

Fig 6.2
The colour wheel.

Let us take the example of a red surface. In the spectrum, red sits between blue and yellow, so it is also able to reflect some blue light and some yellow light, and it will depend how much of either of these other colours it is reflecting as to how dominant the red is, or whether it will be blue biased or yellow biased.

The colour wheel (see Fig 6.2) may appear simplistic, but as an introduction to colour relationships, it tells you what you need to know.

The three primary colours (red, yellow and blue) can, in principle, be mixed to give any other colour except black and white, which are brought into the equation further on. You can see from the colour wheel that by mixing a colour with the one next to it in the circle, we create a new, named colour and its first name will describe its bias. Let's follow an example through.

Mix red and yellow. The result is orange. Now mix orange and yellow. By varying the quantities in the mix, you can achieve a yellow-biased orange, or an orange-biased yellow. If you mix orange and red, you will have an orange-biased red or a red-biased orange.

As you can see from the wheel, orange, yellow and green are side by side, showing that they are close relations and therefore compatible together. They will appear visually as toning, peaceful, and agreeable. You will also see that orange is opposite blue and, because of this, these colours will be of greatest contrast if placed together. In the same way, red contrasts with green, and violet contrasts with yellow.

Relating this to your turned work, you will quickly see that by using red and orange on the same piece the colour change will be subtle, but red and green will provide contrast. Hence the wheel is a useful aid in selecting the sort of effect you are seeking.

Colour can also help to create illusions, by using blues, which tend to be cold colours, and reds which project warmth, although this is only a guideline and is not categorically correct for every blue or every red – this will depend on their bias.

As we have previously established, there are biases to many colours. Even pigments can be biased, so don't be misled by the name a manufacturer attaches to a given dye or stain. The base pigment may be different, giving colour variation between makes bearing the same colour name. This means that when mixing dyes or stains you may not be able to get the exact colour you have in mind, but by trying different manufacturers' products, you may find the hue you require. The problem is really caused by the limited number of pigments which are used in making dyes and stains for the woodworker.

An increasingly complete and comprehensive range of colours is available from artists' paints. You can select pigmented paints and mix the intermediate colours yourself. A wide range of colours is also available from the DIY ranges of paints, the disadvantage being that paints are opaque, whereas dyes are transparent.

With the exception of small, detailed turned items such as lace bobbins, or where you wish to describe detailed pictures or patterns in opaque lines on the wood, dyes are the best medium for *embellishing* wood without obliterating the grain.

You can enlarge your range of dyes by adding inks, food dyes, leather dyes and fabric dyes to your store cupboard, and compromising on any loss of 'light fastness' or handling properties these dyes may impart.

In order to avoid a hit and miss approach to colouring your first pieces, increase your familiarity with colour mixing by treating yourself to a water-colouring pad and acquiring a box of paints together with a couple of small brushes. Then make a colour wheel as previously described by mixing colours in the palette, and then filling in the areas. It is also worthwhile using primary colours and then mixes, to create a linear rainbow to represent the colour spectrum shown in Fig 6.1. As you make such home-made colouring charts, note the colour names and manufacturers' names that you have used. This will be invaluable information in the future.

Blacks and whites

When white is added to a colour in varying amounts, the colour becomes a **tint** or pastel colour. When black is added to a colour, it is known as a **shade**. A **tone** is arrived at by adding grey (a mixture of black and white in any strength) to a colour.

To gain experience in the use of black and white colours, try drawing a line of six 1in (25mm) or ½in (13mm) squares on your pad and, starting at one end, colour the first square white. Add increasing amounts of black, colouring the next four squares with intermediate shades of grey, finishing with black in the final square (see Fig 6.3).

Top **Fig 6.3**
From white to black.

Centre **Fig 6.4**
From red to black.

Above **Fig 6.5**
From red to white.

Now do the same with a spectrum colour. Start with a pure colour, say red, and add small amounts of black, filling in each square with the results, making even gradations to the final black square (see Fig 6.4). Then try adding white, until in half a dozen splodges you have moved from red through dark pink, mid pink and pale pink to white (see Fig 6.5).

Another painting exercise which you may find helpful to extend your experience of how colours work together is to pencil some 3in (76mm) squares with a 1in (25mm) square in each centre, or if you prefer, circles of similar dimensions. Select two primary colours and paint the large area with one of these and the smaller area with the other. Alongside, paint the same colours in reverse proportions. Then move on to contrasting colours and neighbouring ones, each in turn, to complete the experiment (see Fig 6.6). You will notice what completely different effects can be obtained when employing this technique, and this will help you to fully appreciate the significance of these proportions when they are applied to a piece of turned work. With this small amount of background knowledge, the paint palette and the range of dye colours should become less intimidating, and more comprehensible.

Fig 6.6
Examples of the different effects of proportionally larger and smaller amounts of the same colours. Here, you can see the primary colours red and yellow, and red and blue, along with a primary and a secondary colour working together (yellow and green).

Applying colour to your work

When 'painting' with a dye, stain or paint on turned wood, brushes and basic painting ideas and techniques are very useful. I use my sketch pad to try out painting techniques as well as colour combinations, especially if working on a specific design or repeated pattern.

When painting a continuous line or a progressive pattern on a piece, it is always best to support the brush hand either on the work itself, flexing the wrist, or by using a mahlstick on which to support the wrist and from which it can pivot. Both these techniques will stabilise the tip of the brush and prevent shaking which could result in uneven edges or wandering lines of colour.

A blank page in the sketch book is not always a welcome sight. It is sometimes encouraging to lay on a light wash of colour first, either to a specific area or all over the page. When the wash is dry, this coloured undertone may be sufficient to help your ideas flow more easily. Whatever you begin with, unless you are an experienced artist, don't get bogged down with too much detail. Just concentrate on brush strokes of colour to gain an effect; they are usually the most effective.

Once you have a reference for colours and ideas established in your sketch book, you can use your knowledge to great advantage in the workshop. When someone picks out a colour from your charts for the lamp you are making them, you will have a pretty good idea of how to find it or mix it. But note that dye and stain colour samples found on the supplier's shelf are frequently depicted on a uniform, almost white softwood. Don't be misled by the clarity of the colour, which could appear very different on, say, a mahogany bowl.

CHAPTER 7

Dyes and stains

I am often asked 'what is the difference between a dye and a stain?' The terms do tend to cause confusion, and people generally use whichever term they feel comfortable with, without knowledge of the exact definition. It is therefore worth devoting more time to these materials, which were briefly discussed in Chapter 2.

So, briefly, let's go to source material. A nineteenth-century cabinetmaker's guide states that 'stain differs from dye inasmuch as it penetrates just below the surface of the wood instead of colouring its substance throughout'. However, further reading makes it clear that the writer is referring to veneers, which, if soaked for long enough, would be dyed right through. He later underlines the basic difference: that dyes will change the colour of the wood, while stains cover the wood with a thin layer of colouring matter. This statement underlines the inescapable fact that dyes are soluble and pigments are held in suspension.

Dictionary definitions clarify matters further. **A stain** is defined as a liquid preparation used to colour wood, differing from paint by being thinner and being absorbed into the pores of the material instead of forming a coating. **To stain** is to colour by application of pigment that more or less penetrates the substance. A pigment is a finely ground insoluble organic or inorganic substance. It is mixed with a binder and carrier which may be spirit or water. Therefore, a stain will only

penetrate minimally as the pigment only covers the surface of the wood. The use of insoluble pigments leads to the obscuring of the grain of the wood to varying extents ranging from imperceptible to unacceptable.

A dye is defined as a soluble organic or inorganic substance which can be dissolved in spirit or water depending on the choice of carrier. **To dye** is to 'impregnate with colour', although to what extent is not specified. A dye solution penetrates the wood and can be regarded as colouring the substance of the wood. Dyes provide the greatest clarity of colour, and scratches need to be relatively deep before revealing undyed wood.

On occasion, commercial labelling promotes stains which are actually dyes and dyes which contain pigments! In practice, I note that many people refer to wood colours as stains and spectrum colours as dyes. Perhaps this issue of terminology is a good topic for discussion by woodturning groups around the country – it might at least help to alleviate some of the confusion!

The ideal colouring medium for the woodturner needs to:

- Colour the wood without obliterating the grain.
- Penetrate the fibres of the wood.
- Be light fast.
- Be easily controlled.
- Not bleed into the finish applied over it.

Although there will always be compromises with any choice of product which tries to be all things to all men, I find water-based dyes and stains the most suitable for my work, for the following reasons:

- Water is cheap and readily available.
- It is non-flammable, non-toxic and odourless.
- It is an excellent carrier for the dyes themselves and is highly suitable for pigment dispersion.
- It produces solutions of the highest light fastness.

I find the fact that water-based products are slow drying compared with other types of dye and stain to be advantageous in terms of the ease of application, but for those whose personal preference is spirit dyes, read on, try them out, but be aware of the complications and limitations involved in using them. If you find they suit your situation and type of work then by all means use them instead of water-based dyes. The choice of which type of dye or stain to use depends partly on the job in hand and partly on personal preference.

Acrylic, water-based stains

Acrylic, water-based stains are ideal for the newcomer to wood colouring, as they are safe, easy to handle, water soluble, and come in an excellent range of colours (see Fig 7.1). The addition of acrylic resin also significantly reduces the grain raising effect. This obviates the need to carry out the grain raising technique already described. However, on turned pieces where the grain raising procedure is easily carried out, nothing is lost by continuing to practise the technique.

The presence of the acrylic resin slows down the absorption rate, and enables an even coverage of stain over a dry surface without overlap marks. This is a major advantage on larger areas, such as platters or table legs, let alone table tops and cupboard doors. You will notice that I refer to them as 'stains'. I do this to clarify the fact that here we are talking about pigments. These are exceedingly finely ground and mixed together with acrylic resin, using water as the carrier. Penetration of the fibres is not great, but I have found it to be perfectly adequate. The fact that these stains are available in white means that apart from the pastel shades which are ready to use, any other pastel shade can be achieved, using white

Fig 7.1
A stool coloured with black acrylic water-based stain, and limed for extra effect.

together with the vibrant colours. Likewise, by mixing any of the vibrant colours with black, you can darken their appearance, as discussed in Chapter 6.

There is also a complete range of acrylic water-based wood colours available. These too are intermixable to create a vast range of colours and intermediate hues. Remember, as long as the carrier is the same – in this case water – then stains can be mixed with one another.

Water-based dyes

When used with a compatible finish, water-based dyes only fail one of the criteria required for an ideal colouring medium: they raise the grain. However, this problem is readily overcome using the grain raising technique (see page 54).

Light fastness
The light fastness of water-based dyes is extremely good, but cannot be ensured categorically for a specific period of time. Apart from the nature of the dye itself, which may be organic or inorganic, there are several other criteria which come into play, such as whether the dyed wood will be kept in direct sunlight, moved around on a regular basis, or subjected to extensive handling. Damp also has an influence, as will whether the piece is to be kept indoors or outdoors. The light fastness of water-based dyes is significantly reduced out of doors, but indoors, they have the best fastness and are generally better than solvent soluble dyes.

When considering light fastness, I think many people overlook the fact that the natural mellowing of timber over a long period of time can decidedly alter the colour achieved when the wood was freshly cut and dyed. No matter how light fast a dye may be, it will most certainly be affected by the continuous bombardment of ultra-violent light. An ultra-violet absorber spray will provide protection for a considerable time.

Handling

Water-based dyes are undoubtedly the easiest to handle and control. They are available prepared and ready to use, but you may prefer to purchase them in concentrated powder form and dilute them according to the manufacturer's instructions. With experience, the dilution can be varied a little for individual requirements. For instance, a stronger solution is more suitable for painting patterns or pictures, whereas a weaker solution is ideal for a background wash. They are also all intermixable so that, by using the information from the colour charts, it is possible to produce a very wide range of intermediate colours (see Fig 7.2). Available wood colours include antique pine, shades of oak, mahogany, walnut

Fig 7.2
An example of the wide range of colours which can be achieved using water-based dyes. Here they were used to colour this artistic interpretation of water lilies. This piece is approximately 18in(457mm) in diameter and 16in(406mm) high.

and ebony. The spectrum colours are generally variations of red, blue, green and yellow.

As all water dyes and stains are intermixable by virtue of their common carrier, it is possible to mix and match virtually any colour, bearing in mind, of course, that different timbers will react with the dye to produce differing shades of the same colour.

Wood is a living cellular structure, every part of every tree having a unique make-up and each species being different from any other. Perhaps, therefore, it is fairly understandable that, unlike dyeing a man-made fibre of regular content, each piece of wood will react to or take up colour differently from any other. So if you take a batch of blue dye and colour pieces made from six different species of timber or even six different pieces from the same tree, it will not necessarily follow that you will have a perfectly matching set of articles from the point of view of colour. The production of a matching group of turned pieces will be noticeably more difficult when using delicate colours in tones and shades, whereas a uniform black is much more easily achieved.

Unpredictable changes may occur in the appearance of the colour between palette and wood. It may also be affected by chemicals in the water with which the dye is mixed. Even rain-water can now hold a measurable acidity level. The most consistent results will be achieved by mixing with distilled water, and perfectionists may choose to use this.

The physical penetration of water-based dye is not particularly great, and usually wood can only absorb two or three applications. It is therefore important to mix the colours in the palette rather than on the wood, at least until some experience has been gained. A second coat of the same colour dye will intensify the colour, but repeated applications will not continue to improve the depth of colour. Persisting in applying repeated layers of dye will mean that when the dried piece is rubbed back with fine steel wool, a cloud of dried dye powder will be lifted from the revolving piece. This is all the dehydrated dye, which could not be absorbed by the wood, and so simply sits on the surface.

One of the main advantages of water-based dyes is that they are easily controlled, and there are basically two ways of applying them to wood. One is to apply the dye to a dampened surface in order to get an even coverage over a large area – the term large being relative to the total area of the turned item. The other is to apply the dye to a dry surface either direct on to wood or on top of a coat of dry dye.

Good quality flat brushes and pots of clean water, together with a divided palette into which to decant appropriate amounts of dye are the basic requirements for dyeing. Remember, never to dip the brush into the original pots of dye, or from one pot to another, and always wash brushes between colours.

Spirit-based dyes

Spirit dyes are obtainable ready to use, and can be methylated spirit and/or white spirit based. They are also available in powder form, or as a liquid concentrate to be diluted or added in small quantities to ready-made spirit dyes to alter or strengthen their colour. The colour range of spirit dyes varies according to the manufacturer but includes yellow, orange, red, green, blue, black and a huge range of wood colours.

In terms of my own colouring work, I have found spirit dyes difficult to control (here I would define control as being the capacity to provide even coverage over a given area) because, as the spirit carrier is taken up immediately on contact with the wood fibres, it makes even coverage of larger areas without overlap marks and tramlines quite tricky, although this problem can be overcome to an extent by lightly dampening the surface of the work with water before applying the dye.

However, spirit-based dyes are very effective on small,

clearly defined areas, where immediate and intense absorption is required. They are ideal in this context on close-grained woods, although their light fastness may not be as good as that of water-based dyes (see Fig 7.3). A further drawback is that they are flammable and toxic, as well as being totally unsuitable on work that has anything to do with children or food. They demand the safe storage of an adequate supply of white spirit in the workshop for diluting, mixing and brush cleaning, not only when a piece of work is finished but also between colours.

Fig 7.3
The close grain of sycamore is an ideal medium for fine line painting with spirit dyes. This plate and solid form are good examples of sycamore being used in this way.

You will also need a container in which to collect the dirty cleaning spirit; do ensure a safe method of disposal. The cleaning spirit needs to be renewed often, as even small amounts of dye left in the brush can affect the next colour into which the brush is dipped. The darker spirit dyes are very searching and intense, and not easily removed.

When preparing to use spirit dyes in the workplace, decant the required amounts into a divided ceramic palette or pot lids. Beware of using *anything* plastic as the spirit may melt some plastics and severely change the character of others.

All spirit dyes are intermixable, enabling you to increase the colour range to suit your individual requirements. It is best to mix in the palette and then try out the result on scrap timber of the same variety and composition as the piece to be coloured. Colours can then be adjusted before application.

As with water-based dyes, don't be tempted to use spirit dyes direct from their containers. One slip of concentration and an uncleaned brush used for ebony dye, dipped into the tin of yellow dye, will completely ruin the whole tin of yellow.

If you are only using two or three different colours at any one time, try to keep a separate brush for each colour. This helps enormously to keep colours clear and is a useful tip when using any type of dye.

Regardless of any difficulties encountered in their handling and application, spirit dyes do have their place, but my own view is that they are of greater value to the cabinetmaker than to the woodturner.

CHAPTER 8

Single-colour application

Applying an acrylic water-based stain

Project
Ash Stool

Let us look at a specific project. As discussed on page 36 in Chapter 3, an ash stool is a good project for colouring with an acrylic stain (see Fig 8.1).

Fig 8.1
The ash stool turned and coloured for this project.

Turning

First select a 1in (25mm) thick, 10in (254mm) diameter ash blank, or cut one from a straight-grained light coloured ash board. Decide which is the best side for the top of the stool and mark the centre point on the reverse side with a bodkin. Drill a hole with a suitable sized drill bit ready for mounting the blank on the screw chuck.

The next step is to mount a 6in (152mm) diameter faceplate on to the headstock, and stick double sided tape around its outer edge (see Fig 8.2). Holding the ash blank with the left hand, bring up the tailstock with a revolving centre and locate it in the centre hole you have drilled (see Fig 8.3). As you tighten up the tailstock, the double sided tape will obligingly grip on to the top side of the stool creating a reassuring grip on the blank.

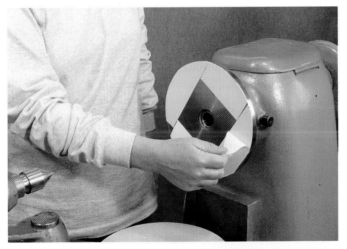

Fig 8.2
Attach double-sided tape around the outer edge of the faceplate.

Fig 8.3
Bring up the tailstock and locate it in the hole you have drilled.

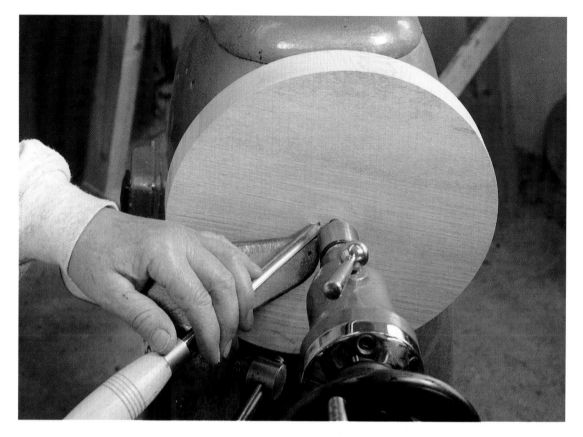

Fig 8.4
Use a shallow fluted gouge to
reach the centre of the work
without fouling the live centre.

You can now safely true up the outer edge of the disc
and then, with the tool rest parallel with the face of the
disc and as close to it as possible, face off the work with
a deep fluted gouge. You will need to use a shallow
fluted gouge with swept back wings to reach the centre
of the work without fouling the live centre (see Fig 8.4).

Finish the flat face of the work with increasingly fine
abrasives, say from 120 through to 320, to achieve a really
good finish. Even though this side of the stool may never
be seen, it's nice to know it has been well finished, and
of course you will be able to feel the surface when you
pick it up.

At this point carry out the grain raising technique as
described in the section on preparation (see page 54)
before finally finishing with Grade 0000 steel wool and a
tack cloth.

If you wish to colour the underside of the stool top,
now is the easiest time to do it, by following the

technique I describe in a moment for the upper surface.

Take the stool top off the lathe and put it to one side while exchanging the faceplate for a screw chuck. Now mount the stool top on the screw chuck. If the screw is unnecessarily long for the thickness of the wood use a packing piece of say a ¼in (6mm) thick disc of ply with a screw hole in the centre. In other words, a large wooden washer (see Fig 8.5).

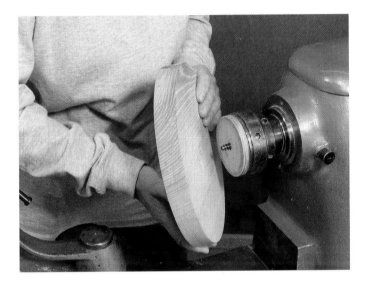

Above left **Fig 8.5**
Mounting the stool top on the screw chuck with the help of a wooden 'washer' to reduce the screw length.

Above **Fig 8.6**
Tapering the edge so that it is narrower towards the underside of the seat will visually reduce the bulk of the stool without affecting its strength.

Make sure the stool top is mounted and screwed on tightly, firmly and evenly. Now make a few passes across the face to make a stool seat that is slightly dished for comfort, or flat if it is to be used more often for tea-cups! I prefer to taper the edge, making it narrower towards the underside (see Fig 8.6). This visually reduces the bulk of the stool while removing none of its strength.

Finish the piece with abrasives and steel wool as before. Carry out the grain raising technique again before making a final pass with the tack cloth to ensure a clean surface.

Now drill the holes for the stool legs. For the greatest stability, the area covered by the foot of the legs should be a little larger than the diameter of the stool top. In order to obtain the same angle for each hole it is necessary to make a wedge-shaped jig for use with the pillar drill (see Fig 8.7). For a 10in (254mm) diameter stool I suggest a ¾in

(19mm) diameter hole. At the same time, make a gauge for sizing the tops of the legs by drilling a hole of the same size and depth in a piece of scrap wood. Mark on it what it is for and the size of the hole and keep it handy. By drilling the leg holes at this stage, any marks or accidental damage caused between lathe and pillar drill can be attended to before applying the colour.

Before opening any cans of stain in readiness for the colouring procedure, clean the dust off the lathe and surrounding flat surfaces. Unless you have an extractor system, you may raise quite a lot of dust, so give it time to settle or blow away before colouring begins. For further details refer to Chapter 5 on preparation.

Fig 8.7
Drilling the holes for the legs using the pillar drill. Note the wedge-shaped jig which ensures the holes are all drilled at the same angle.

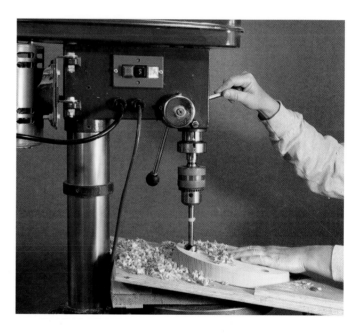

Colouring

Carefully remount the stool seat on the screw chuck and check the finish. If all is well select your can of acrylic water-based stain. It comes ready to use, but shake the can well before decanting an appropriate amount for the stool top into a palette large enough to facilitate the use of a sponge applicator. Only experience will tell you how much stain is required for any particular job. If you have a selection of applicator sizes from which to choose, the

Left **Fig 8.8**
Decanting the stain into a suitable palette. Note the two sponge applicators. The larger of these will be used to remove surplus acrylic from the work (see Fig 8.10).

Below **Fig 8.9**
Spread the colour firmly on to the wood, working briskly and keeping only one wet edge.

2in (51mm) would be a good choice for the flat face of the stool top, and the 1in (25mm) ideal for the rim of the top and the legs (see Fig 8.8).

Fill the applicator with the stain and, with bold strokes, firmly spread the colour on to the wood, working fairly quickly from one side of the stool top to the other, keeping only one wet edge (see Fig 8.9). This technique is a good working principle to establish when applying a liquid product to any sizeable piece of work, so start practising it from the beginning. Neatly colour the rim of the stool top using the smaller applicator. The wood will absorb the water carrying the pigment, but it cannot absorb the acrylic element which has now served its purpose, so it is necessary to wipe off the surplus acrylic from the surface of the work. Do this with a clean dry sponge applicator, working always in the direction of the grain (see Fig 8.10). If you remove all the surface excess you will have a tinted colour – a hint of green, for example, as in this case. However, if the colour is not of sufficient depth, then a second coat can be applied in exactly the same manner. You need not wait until the first coat is dry, but you do need to cover the whole piece completely. Finishing strokes are made with the grain to lessen the impact of any stray sponge marks which may inadvertently be left on the wood. If these marks are across the grain, they have a greater visual impact and are unacceptable to the eye as is clearly shown in Fig 8.11. Any marks running the length of the grain will be accepted as part of the grain structure.

Below **Fig 8.10**
Remove surplus acrylic using a clean, dry sponge applicator. Always work in the direction of the grain.

Below right **Fig 8.11**
Sponge marks going across the grain create an unsightly and unacceptable effect, as you can see here.

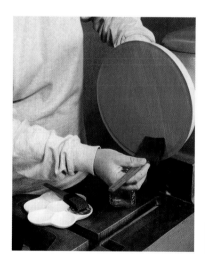

If the surplus acrylic resin is not removed from the surface of the work immediately after application, it will quickly dry where it is left and will invariably give a blotchy appearance. Any finger marks on wet stain will also remain there when it dries, so do be careful.

It is essential to wash out the sponge applicators and palettes as soon as you have finished using them, not only to prevent contamination of other colours but also because, if left to dry out, the water content of the stain will evaporate leaving the acrylic resin to harden. This is then insoluble, so the sponge becomes unusable and the palette a mess.

Drying time depends on the ambient temperature and the amount of stain you have applied to the wood. I prefer to leave it overnight before going on to the finishing stage. Remove the stool top and chuck from the lathe together and put them aside in a dust free zone where the drying process can take place.

In the meantime, cut three pieces of 2in (51mm) square by 11in (279mm) long ash similar in natural colour to the top. Turn them between centres to a similar diameter, and face off both ends. If you haven't already made a sketch or thought about the shape of the legs, now is a good time to do it (see Fig 8.12). If you are short of design ideas, look at other furniture legs for inspiration.

Fig 8.12
Make preliminary sketches or drawings of the legs before you begin turning.

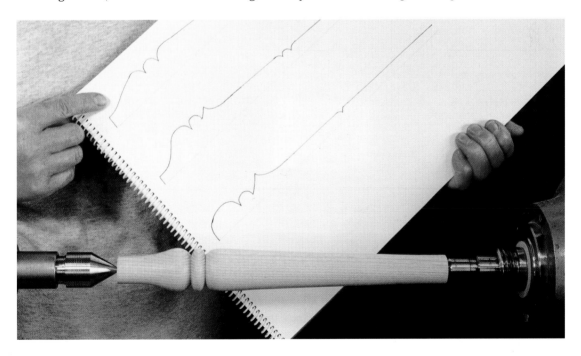

Have a pair of callipers handy, set to the size of the hole into which each leg will fit, and incorporate this slim end into your design (see Fig 8.13). Try the leg for fit using the gauge you made at the outset – depth as well as diameter need to be right (see Fig 8.14). Make your first leg and then, with a little help from a rule, a pair of callipers and a keen pair of eyes, make the other two to match. Remember, the important part is the fit of the leg in the hole – don't forget you need room for a drop of glue too.

Below left **Fig 8.13**
Use callipers to check the
diameter is correct.

Below right **Fig 8.14**
Checking the leg for fit.

Bottom **Fig 8.15**
Applying the stain along the work,
with the grain.

Follow your tool finish with a few passes of abrasive, steel wool and tack cloth, and then apply the grain raising technique once more. Using the same procedure as before, apply the acrylic stain to each leg in turn. This time work from one end to the other, remembering to remove the excess acrylic and make finishing strokes with the grain (see Fig 8.15). It is not necessary to dye that part of the leg which is the joint for the top. This undyed end is just long enough to enable you to remove the leg neatly from the lathe without fingering the stain, and stand it up on a flat surface to dry.

Below **Fig 8.16**
Steel wool and the tack cloth prepare the leg for finishing.

Bottom **Fig 8.17**
Applying the finish: in this case a tung oil based product.

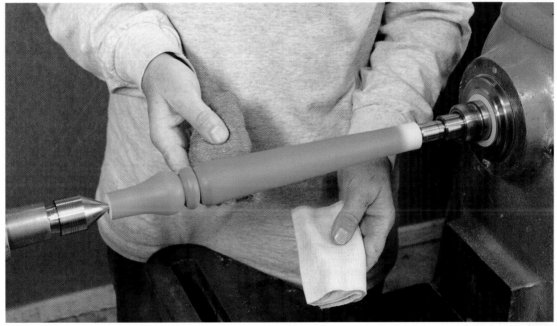

To finish the parts of the stool, remount each one on the lathe in turn, and lightly rub over with fine steel wool followed by the tack cloth (see Fig 8.16). For a hardwearing, water- and stainproof finish apply three coats of one of the tung based products described in Chapter 2, allowing an adequate drying time between coats and rubbing back lightly with fine steel wool each time (see Fig 8.17).

A light coat of neutral wax polish will provide an attractive finish before gluing the pieces together using a

good quality wood glue applied to the hole. Make sure the legs are fully in their holes before leaving the glue to set (see Figs 8.18 and 8.19).

If you choose to mix your own colour of acrylic stain from more than one of the ready to use colours, be sure to mix sufficient for the whole project and keep it in an airtight container between stages. White liming wax can be used over acrylic stains to fill the grain, and the combination produces a pleasing effect. Liming techniques are described in Chapter 14.

Below **Fig 8.18**
Applying a coat of neutral wax polish.

Below right Fig **8.19**
Gluing the pieces together with wood glue.

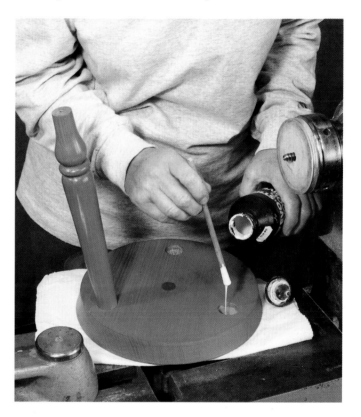

Applying a water-based dye

As with any project, the choice of wood depends on the intended final result. For example, for a single colour piece, a close- or even-grained wood will produce the best results because it will give a complete surface finish, not broken up by too coarse an open grain. Let's look at the processes for making a simple vase (see Fig 8.20).

Project
Vase

Fig 8.20
The iroko vase made and
coloured in this project.

Turning

There is obviously a variety of shapes you could make for
this project, but the one I have chosen depicts what to
my mind are the essential elements for a successful
colouring project. They are: simplicity of design,
balance, and style. Running alongside these is the
standard of wood finish and the choice of colour.

Mount a piece of wood 3in (76mm) square by 8in
(203mm) long between centres. I used iroko – but maple
or top quality ash would be equally suitable.

Turn a cylinder to the greatest diameter the wood will
allow. Face off the ends, and turn down a spigot to marry
with the 2in (51mm) spigot chuck so that you can mount
the piece for end-grain turning (see Figs 8.21, 8.22 and 8.23).

It doesn't matter if you have a different chucking
system from me, as long as you can hold the work

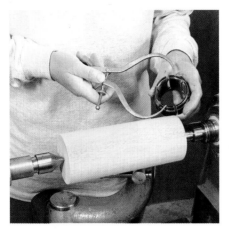

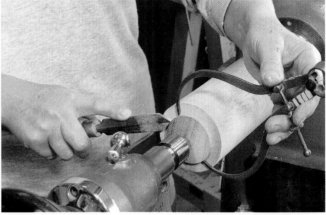

Above **Fig 8.21**
Turn a cylinder to the greatest diameter the blank will allow, and face off the ends. Then set the callipers to the exact diameter of a 2in (51mm) spigot chuck.

Above right **Fig 8.22**
Hold the callipers with your left hand as a gauge while you cut a spigot using a diamond parting tool.

Right **Fig 8.23**
The spigot should fit accurately into the dovetailed recess of the spigot chuck.

without using the tailstock. The reason for this is to enable the use of a Jacobs chuck and bit in the tailstock.

Switch on the lathe at its lowest speed, bring up the drill bit in the tailstock and, using it as a horizontal pillar drill, drill a ¼in (6mm) diameter hole in the vase as deep as the drill bit will allow without penetrating the bottom (see Fig 8.24). Even though the lathe is running at its slowest speed while drilling, withdraw the bit frequently, drilling short lengths at a time so that it neither becomes stuck nor overheats the wood or the drill.

Remove the chuck from the tailstock, and return the lathe to normal speed. Then, with the tool rest across the end grain of the wood, and working from the outside edge to the centre with a small deep fluted gouge, turn the bell of the interior of the neck (see Fig 8.25). Be sure to make a continuous flowing line. I make the final cuts with a shallow fluted gouge, allowing the flute to feather

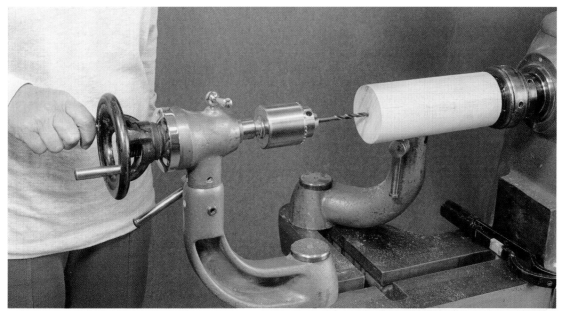

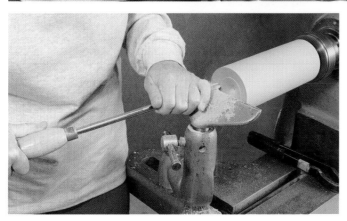

Top and Above **Fig 8.24**
Drilling a ¼in (6mm) diameter hole in the vase as deep as the drill bit will allow, without penetrating the bottom. The Jacobs chuck and bit allow you to use the lathe as a 'horizontal pillar drill' for this operation.

Left **Fig 8.25**
Turning the bell of the interior of the vase mouth using a small deep fluted gouge.

out the demarcation between the bell and the drilled hole (see Fig 8.26).

Now turn the tool rest and your attention to the body of the vase. With the exception of the V area between the body and the foot, I suggest you used a small deep fluted gouge throughout. For the V area I used the pointed end of the skew, and made final cuts with the heel of the skew blending in the shape of the bulbous body towards the V above the foot (see Fig 8.27). You will see that I left a shoulder of about ⅜in (10mm) for parting off when the vase was complete (see Fig 8.28).

After sanding the vase lightly with progressively finer grits and, finishing with 320 grit for a beautiful finish, go through the grain raising technique as described on page 54. The work is now ready for colouring.

Right **Fig 8.26**
Feathering out the demarcation between the bell and the drilled hole using a shallow fluted gouge.

Below right **Fig 8.27**
I chose to use an oval skew chisel to make the finishing cuts along the body of the vase and into the V above the foot.

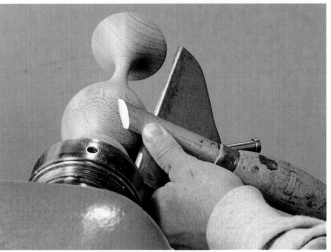

Fig 8.28
I left a ⅜in (10mm) shoulder for parting off once the vase was complete.

Colouring

Decant a reasonable amount of your chosen colour dye into a palette – about a tablespoon should do. Any natural colouring needs to be taken into account when selecting wood for a turned piece to be dyed with just one colour. Naturally occurring patches of darker wood may be better under a darker more intense dye, which will reduce their impact, or a pale colour which will accentuate them. It is a case of choosing whichever you feel is appropriate for a given piece.

Have readily available a brush, pots of brush cleaning water and a disposal bucket and, most importantly, a clean damp sponge for dampening the surface of the wood before applying the colour. The reason for this is that the dye is, to all intents and purposes, coloured water. If it were applied to a dry wood surface, huge amounts of dye would be absorbed where the brush hit the work, which would mean only a short brush stroke before the brush would need replenishing. The second brush full of dye, applied alongside the first, would leave a clearly defined overlap mark. It would be virtually impossible to blend the two together to make an even coverage, especially bearing in mind that, on a turned piece of work, all curved surfaces are displaying varying angles of end grain. Between these and the areas of side

Below **Fig 8.29**
Dampening the surface of the piece with a sponge so as to assist the water-based solution to spread evenly across the fibres.

Below right **Fig 8.30**
Paint on the dye in long, flowing strokes along the vase, reloading the brush as required.

Bottom left **Fig 8.31**
The random, speckled effect which can be caused by the leaching effect of capillary action through the wood is shown here on a decorative flower approximately 2½in (64mm) in diameter, turned from green holly.

grain there will be enormous variation in the rate of absorption of the dye. Take into consideration too the varying densities of wood in any one piece and perhaps you can envisage the uneven coverage of colour that could occur. The solution is therefore to dampen the surface of the work with a damp sponge (see Fig 8.29). This should not be so wet that it dilutes the colour, but damp enough to assist the water-based solution to spread evenly across the fibres.

Leave the vase mounted on the lathe for colouring purposes, but apply the dye while the work is stationary, revolving it by hand as necessary to make all parts accessible to the brush. Load your brush – for this size of work

Right **Fig 8.32**
Colouring the open bell of the vase.

I would use a ¾in (19mm) or 1in (25mm) flat lacquer brush – and starting at the base of the vase, paint in long flowing strokes along the body towards the neck, reloading the brush as required and spreading the dye to obtain as even a coverage as possible without runs (see Fig 8.30). Finishing strokes should be with the grain.

When applying the dye to a thin wall, whether it is that of the flared neck of a vase, a bowl or decorative item, leaching caused by capillary action can occur. This may cause a random speckled effect on the opposite side of the wood, which in some cases may be acceptable (see Fig 8.31). However, if it is not, the best solution is to use the same colour dye on both sides of the piece. So, with the same dye, colour the open bell of the vase, again following the grain for the final brush strokes (see Fig 8.32). If you have left a rim at the periphery of the neck, make sure that it is coloured too. If you wish to strengthen the colour with a second coat, apply this while the piece is still damp, so that it too is assisted in covering the surface evenly. Do not be tempted to 'touch-in' with the second coat, as this will always show up when the dye is dry. Always cover the piece completely with each coat.

Wash out your brush and wait for the vase to dry. Drying time will depend on the weather, time of year, workshop temperature and the amount of moisture absorbed by the wood during the preparation and dyeing process. Overnight is a sensible minimum drying time and 24 hours or longer even better.

When the vase is completely dry, remount it on the lathe. If you removed it from the spigot chuck in the meantime and now find a little difficulty in getting it to run exactly true, don't worry. For the purposes of finishing, a slight eccentricity will be of no consequence. Brushes and polishing cloths will absorb the inaccuracy of the surface, and the shoulder for parting off close to the headstock will undoubtedly be true enough.

Rub back the dyed wood very lightly with fine steel wool taking care not to use much pressure on those areas

Below **Fig 8.33**
Rub back lightly with fine steel wool, followed by the tack cloth.

Below right **Fig 8.34**
Use a pad of soft paper to apply a coat of sanding sealer to the stationary work.

of side grain. Follow with the tack cloth (see Fig 8.33). Then, with a pad of soft paper, apply a coat of sanding sealer to the stationary work, covering the surface evenly (see Fig 8.34). Allow this to dry, in line with the manufacturer's instructions.

Above **Fig 8.35**
Applying wax polish with a brush, first to the revolving and then to the stationary work, ensuring all the open grain is properly coated.

Above right **Fig 8.36**
Buffing the work using a buffing brush, for maximum shine. A final buff should then be performed with a safety cloth.

Now make another pass with fine steel wool and the tack cloth, and the vase will be ready for a coat of polish. Brush a coat of neutral wax polish on to the revolving piece – I use a clean 1in (25mm) paint brush for this. Buff up the finish with another brush and use a safety cloth for the final polish (see Figs 8.35 and 8.36). If you prefer a gloss finish, then a pass along the revolving work with a carnauba block will do the trick.

All that's left to do now is the difficult bit – getting the work off the lathe without it flying through the window, ripping itself out of the spigot or turning itself inside out. This is my method, which has so far worked every time!

Refer to Fig 8.37 (which continues on page 94). First, fold up a piece of soft paper about 2in (51mm) square, and hold it across the mouth of the vase while you bring

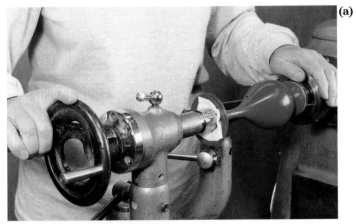 (a)

 (b)

 (c)

From top to bottom **Fig 8.37**
Removing the work from the lathe.
(a) Bring up the tailstock, protecting the mouth of the vase with a piece of soft paper.
(b) Begin the cut using a diamond parting tool, leaving a ¼in (6mm) spigot.
(c) Make the final parting cut close to the work.

up the tailstock with the revolving centre. Tighten it up firmly, but avoid a great deal of pressure on the vase. I use a diamond parting tool, but a straight- sided or hollow ground tool will be fine as long as it is *really* sharp. I like a long bevel on mine to give a good, slightly concave cut across most of the spigot. This will ensure that the vase will stand without rocking when taken off the lathe. However, I withdraw it leaving about ¼in (6mm) diameter spigot still on the vase, and exchange it for another tool; an 8in (203mm) length of disused industrial hacksaw blade, with the teeth ground off and one end shaped into a miniature parting tool. With this I make those last few cuts through the spigot. I make perhaps six small cuts side by side, leading with the cut nearest the headstock, the final parting cut being close to the work. As it is severed, the vase rolls gently into my supporting left hand. With my right hand I push away the tailstock, then safely lift the work clear and switch off the lathe. The tiny pip on the bottom can be hand-sanded off. Dye, sealer and polish will complete the project!

Right and below **Fig 8.37**
(d) Sever the work so that it comes gently away from the lathe into the hand.
(e) Hand-sand the remaining tiny pip on the base of the vase.

(d)

(e)

CHAPTER 9

Colour blending

I t can be most effective to use two or more colours on a piece of work. The blending technique is used where no clearly delineated areas of colour are desired, but rather a more natural merging of one colour with the next. This can be done in any plane – horizontal, vertical, or diagonal. It can be used successfully on a multi-section piece of turnery, on spindlework, or on bowls and platters (see Fig 9.1).

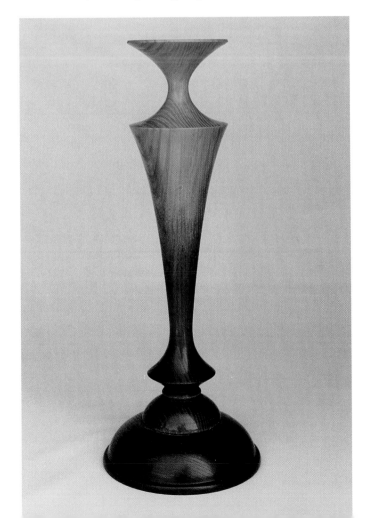

Fig 9.1
An example of colour blending using yellow and blue to produce a 'transition' area of green on this vase.

Practise first on a cylinder or some other uncomplicated profile of approximately 3in (76mm) diameter and 8in (203mm) long, so that you can master the technique before getting involved with the different rates of absorption and thus differing colour intensities of more complicated designs.

At this stage it is a good idea to remember that your choice of colour is providing an *embellishment* for your work. It is not always necessary to apply it to an elaborate design. Very often the simplest lines respond best to the dramatic change effected by colour, especially when using more than one colour on a piece.

Virtually any timber is suitable, but one with little of its own colour is best. It is still worth preparing a trial piece properly to appreciate the full effect of the blending technique. Inadequate preparation will carry its own message when the dyed results fail to please!

There are three ways in which you can blend the colours. One is to blend parallel with grain, the second is across the direction of the grain, the third is diagonally across the grain. The first is by far the easiest to do and is a good confidence booster.

Method 1

Mount your experimental cylinder between centres on the lathe. Remember that pale-coloured woods will most accurately reflect the palette colours. Hand turn the work to make the part you are working on easily accessible. Don't turn on the lathe while dyeing.

Decant small amounts of two water-based dyes into two clean palettes and have ready a brush for each colour dye. This will help to keep the colours clear. Remember, we want to blend the colours, one with the other *on the wood*, not in the palette. I would suggest selecting two primary colours from the spectrum so that the blended area is quite distinctive. Have in mind some idea of what you are expecting to achieve.

A piece of absorbent paper or safety cloth should be to hand to absorb excess moisture from the brush while you are working, be it dye or brush rinsing water. You will need to be able to control the amount of liquid on the surface of the piece, and dabbing the brush on the absorbent cloth is the best way of doing it.

Dampen the surface of the cylinder with a clean sponge as previously described. Don't make it excessively wet, or at best the colours will be diluted, and at worst will run. I prefer to apply the lighter colour first. Whenever applying more than one colour, it is always easier to cover a light colour with a darker one, but impossible to cover a dark colour with a lighter one.

As an example, use yellow and dark blue. Make two or

Top left **Fig 9.2**
Make two or three brush strokes of the yellow dye along the length of the dampened grain.

Top right **Fig 9.3**
Apply the blue in the same way, moving towards the yellow.

Above left **Fig 9.4**
The last stroke overlaps the yellow, creating a blended area of green.

Above right **Fig 9.5**
With the yellow brush, use lighter strokes to feather the new colour into the yellow side of the work.

three brush strokes of yellow dye the length of the grain (see Fig 9.2). Follow this by taking a brush full of the blue, and starting two or three brush widths away from the yellow, make brush strokes in the same direction, but towards the yellow (see Fig 9.3). The last brush stroke will be *over* the yellow dye, which will of course turn green (see Fig 9.4). A further brush stroke of blue over yellow will make the green band wider. If the blue is visually too dominant in the green, take a yellow brush and go over the green area using lighter strokes to feather the colour towards the yellow side, but always in the direction of the grain (see Fig 9.5).

Fig 9.6
Making a rainbow effect by blending red into yellow to make orange, red into blue to make purple and yellow into blue to make green.

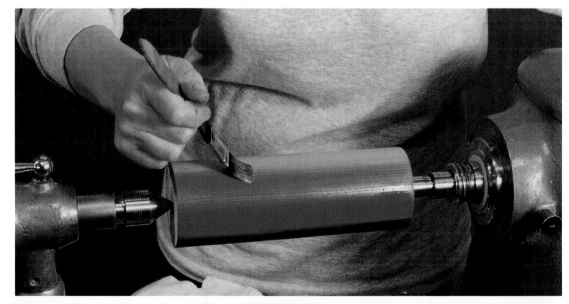

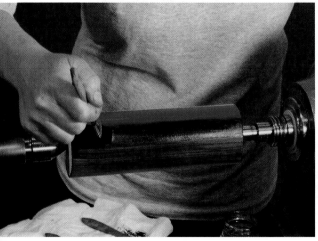

As you are using a cylinder mounted on the lathe, before the surface of the work dries, turn the work towards you and practise the same routine where the colours meet again. You will notice how the colours change when they dry out. For further practice, turn down the cylinder until it is clean and prepare it once more before repeating the experiment. You will probably find that the depth of penetration is about that of a finishing cut. Not a lot but just enough to make a difference!

Now try the same procedure using three dyes. Decant a small amount of red into the palette, next to the yellow and blue, and this time blend red into the yellow to make orange, and red into the blue to make purple. Finally, blend yellow into the blue to make green. Your primary colours have now blended to produce a rainbow effect (see Fig 9.6).

Method 2

Mount another prepared cylinder on the lathe. Have ready yellow and blue, each with its own brush. This time, the blended area is to be across the grain or, if you prefer, around the cylinder. Dampen the surface of the wood, as before. Starting at one end, apply the yellow dye

Below left **Fig 9.7**
Apply the yellow dye along half the length of the dampened cylinder, in a band right around it.

Below **Fig 9.8**
Apply the blue dye from the opposite end, allowing it to cover about 1in (25mm) of the yellow, creating green.

Below and below right **Fig 9.9**
Diagonal application to form
spirals of the two colours,
blending them by a slight overlap
in a similar way to Method 2.

along half the length of the cylinder, but in a band right around it (see Fig 9.7). Take up the brush of blue dye and apply it similarly from the opposite end of the cylinder.

Allow the blue dye to cover about 1in (25mm) of the yellow (see Fig 9.8). Obviously, you can vary this width according to the length of the cylinder or your personal choice, or even by accident! Take up the yellow brush and adjust the resulting area of green with the addition of extra yellow dye. However, do be careful to wipe off the green dye which will appear on your yellow dye brush each time you pull it across the blended area. Self-discipline and brush control are both called for here. A little patience and persistence will be required to achieve the desired effect, but practice will soon make perfect. Once the skill is acquired, it becomes quite feasible to blend many colours on the same piece of work.

Method 3

The third way of blending on the cylinder, or any spindlework, is diagonally, forming a spiral. On the prepared and dampened surface, describe a spiral with a brush load of, say, yellow dye. Make this two or three brush widths. Take a brush load of blue dye and

Above **Fig 9.10**
A further application of yellow over
the blue will widen the green band.

describe a similar shape two or three brush widths away from the yellow, but work towards it until you cover about a width of ½in (13mm) of the yellow band, turning it green (see Fig 9.9). A brush of yellow over the blue will widen the green band (see Fig 9.10). Complete the cylinder using just the two colours before trying another one, blending the three colours in the spiral form. A little practice will enable you to achieve a smooth transition from one colour to the next.

The blending technique can be great fun. It can also be very useful to mask changing directions of grain on the outer surfaces of bowls, and I enjoy using it for the undersides of my pedestal bowls (see Fig 9.11) and my sunset and sunrise platters (see Fig 9.12).

Above **Fig 9.11**
Undersides of two lime pedestal bowls, where the colour blending technique has been used deliberately to accommodate the dye absorbancy discrepancy due to the variation of grain structure.

Below **Fig 9.12**
Colour blending can be used to create a wide range of effects, such as this 'sunset platter', turned from iroko and decorated with a copper gilt edge (for more information on gilding, see Chapter 18).

CHAPTER 10

Grain-guided colouring

In this chapter we look at the possibilities of applying two or more colours to the same piece, without merging them together, using a technique which I developed myself, and have called grain-guided colouring.

This technique uses wild grain formations to define the area to be coloured, so we need to select a timber with a distinct grain marking. By using two or more colours, the natural pattern of the grain is emphasised, and the wilder the grain, the more dramatic the effect. There are other woods suitable for this technique (such as elm or sweet chestnut), but I have found ash to be the most effective. The greatest visual impact of grain-guided colouring can be achieved on a turned platter or shallow bowl.

You could colour a set of such platters from the same plank. With the same colour combination they would have a similar yet random grain, producing related yet totally individual pieces. The technique can of course be applied to spindlework; for example, a pair of table lamps could be dyed to striking effect.

Project Wide-rimmed platter

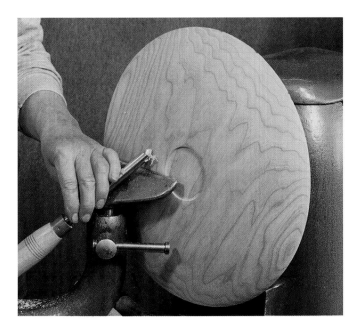

Turning

Try making a wide-rimmed platter from ash or sweet chestnut. A disc 1in (25mm) thick and anywhere between 10in (254mm) and 12in (305mm) diameter will make a platter of sufficient size to be eye-catching. It is also quite feasible to mount it on a shallow-depth screw chuck. Be sure to reduce the lathe speed for turning a blank of this diameter, at least to start with, until you are satisfied that it is balanced and trued.

Turn a shallow dovetail shape recess for a 2in (51mm) or 2½in (64mm) diameter expanding dovetail. To do this, I used a skew chisel and a ¼in (6mm) shallow fluted gouge. The depth of the recess should be kept to a minimum – ¹⁄₁₆in (2mm) is plenty and will look much neater on the finished platter than a deeper one. Make the flat foot around the recess between ½in (13mm) and ¾in (19mm) wide. These measurements are approximate, and will vary according to the overall diameter of the platter.

I prefer not to make too much of a feature of the foot on a platter which is to be decorated. So, from the outer edge of the foot rim, cut a single flowing line to the outer rim of the platter using a ½in (13mm) shallow fluted gouge (see Fig 10.1). Finish with three or four grades of

Fig 10.1
If you prefer not to make too much of a feature of the foot, as I do on work which is to be decorated, cut a single flowing line from the outer edge of the foot to the outer rim, using a shallow fluted gouge.

abrasive, steel wool and tack cloth in the normal way. Apply the grain raising technique, and finish again. Reverse the platter, and turn off the upper surface with a ⅜in (10mm) deep fluted gouge, keeping a simple profile (see Fig 10.2). Complete the preparations with abrasives and grain raising.

The platter should now present a surface displaying a wonderful random grain pattern, any part of which can be followed across its diameter, over the perimeter and across the reverse side, joining up where it meets the face again.

Fig 10.2
Reverse the platter on to an expanding collet chuck . . . and turn off the upper surface using a deep fluted gouge.

Colouring

Nature has provided the pattern, now it is up to the colourist to take advantage of it. Even when using two colours, the choice of exactly which areas to dye with which colour is enormous. To start with, I suggest an approximate 50:50 ratio, applied randomly, but always following the grain-guided area right around the piece – back and front, without changing track. At this stage, I find it easier to remove the platter from the lathe for colouring, and work on a flat bench. This is a personal choice, which may be influenced by lighting, the desire to sit down to do the colouring, or the option of using a small turntable on which to bring the work easily to hand in a horizontal plane. Working on the flat does reduce the risk of the dye running unexpectedly, which could happen if you inadvertently overload the brush and apply it to the vertical face of a platter still mounted on the lathe.

I would suggest colouring the face of the platter first, simply because that is the side which will be viewed more frequently and by starting on this side you will have more control over the colour formation. If you colour the underside first then the bands of colour will be dictated for the top side before you can actually see what is going to happen. When you do it you will see exactly what I mean!

Select two contrasting dye colours for the first attempt, so that you can readily see the areas that you are dyeing. Have three clean brushes ready for use, one for each colour dye and one for water only. The width of the grain to be coloured will dictate the best size of brush. Use a ½in (13mm) or even 1in (25mm) flat brush if there are wide tracts to be covered, and round ended or pointed brushes for finer lines and fiddly bits.

Decant a tablespoonful or thereabouts of the lighter of the two colours into your palette. On the dry upper side of the platter, select an area to colour, bordered on both sides by grain line. The area may simply be between grain lines, or may incorporate one or more lines.

With a clean flat brush dipped in clean water, lightly but meticulously, with a neat edge, dampen the area to be coloured. Go right to the edge of the platter, so that when it comes to colouring the reverse side, you can clearly pick up the correct grain areas for the right colour to give continuity (see Fig 10.3). It is essential not to let the water form any runs across the grain perimeter or the dye will follow them and completely spoil the effect. When you have dampened an area of grain in this way, take a brush full of the lighter of the two colours. Squeeze off the excess dye against the side of the palette and dye over the same area equally carefully. Work systematically from the point furthest away from you, dyeing the dampened areas of wood, neatly following the edge of the annual rings, evenly filling in the area between (see Fig 10.4).

You are in fact following the technique of applying a single colour water-based dye to a dampened surface to get an even spread of colour. Only this time you are controlling its boundaries, stopping the spread of dye by facing it with a dry line.

Repeat the technique for all the light coloured areas, dampening and colouring one or two at a time (see Fig 10.5). However, if the areas you wish to dye are very narrow, or if you decide to colour just the eye of the grain, you will be able to apply the dye without previously dampening the wood.

Allow the first colour to dry before repeating the technique for the second colour (see Fig 10.6). If you don't, you may unwittingly spread coloured fingerprints on to areas where they are not required. When both colours are completely dry, turn the platter over and complete the other side in the same manner, picking up the grain lines and colours at the rim and joining them up across the face of the work.

The colouring may end here, or you may like to run an appropriately coloured felt-tip touch-up pen along the now dry grain lines for extra effect (see Fig 10.7). The pen could be either a complementary or a contrasting colour to the body of the work, as you wish. To complete the piece, rub over gently with grade 0000 steel wool and then apply a suitable finish – I would recommend an oiled and polished finish. In order to avoid any remote possibility of dragging one colour over the next, the oiling (which can be done off the lathe), should follow exactly the same sequence as the colouring (see Fig 10.8).

Now remount the platter for the final polishing (see Fig 10.9). It will not be possible to reach the recess to buff the final polish on the underside while the platter is mounted on a revolving lathe. A successful alternative is to buff with

Opposite top **Fig 10.3**
Dampen the area to be coloured, being sure to go right to the edge of the platter. Note that I have clearly marked my brush for use with water only.

Opposite centre **Fig 10.4**
Colour the area of grain you have just dampened with the lighter of the two colours, working systematically towards you from the point furthest away.

Opposite bottom **Fig 10.5**
Repeat the technique for all the light coloured areas, dampening and colouring one or two at a time.

Above left and above **Fig 10.6**
Allow the lighter colour to dry and then repeat the procedure with the darker colour.

Left **Fig 10.7**
For extra effect you can use a felt-tip touch-up pen to highlight the grain lines.

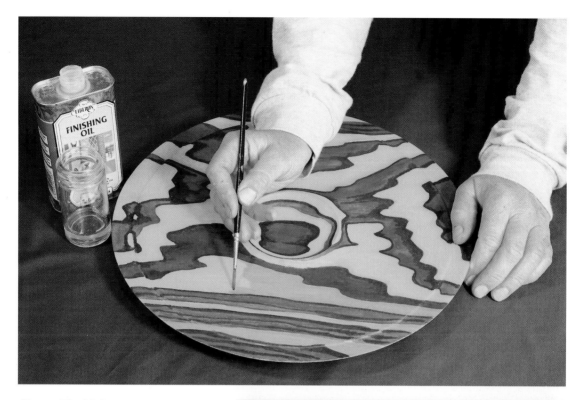

Above **Fig 10.8**
Follow the same sequence when applying the finish as you did when applying the colour.

Right **Fig 10.9**
Remount the work on the lathe for final polishing.

Above left and above **Fig 10.10**
To buff the recess on the underside of the piece, mount a drill brush in a Jacobs chuck fitted to the headstock, brush the polish on to the recess and burnish the finish as shown.

Left **Fig 10.11**
The finished piece.

a round drill brush. To do this, take the platter off the lathe, mount the drill in a Jacobs chuck fitted into the headstock and then, with the polish already brushed on the underside, hold the platter against the revolving brush allowing it to burnish the finish (see Figs 10.10 and 10.11).

Grain-guided colouring can provide an infinite number of effects (see Fig 10.12). It is quite impossible to do two alike, making every piece unique, even if the turned platters or other items are all of the same design.

Fig 10.12
Grain-guided colouring offers a huge range of possible effects, with no two pieces the same.

CHAPTER 11

Painting with dye

A n enormous number of artistic possibilities arise under this heading. Here are two methods you can use to achieve a wide range of effects.

Method 1

The first option is to apply water-based dye to a prepared, but untreated, dry wood surface such as decorative turning or furniture. Using the dye as a painting medium, apply it directly to the prepared wood. If you are mixing powdered dye, it is sometimes advantageous not to dilute it quite as much as the manufacturer suggests. This will make the dye a little less runny, denser in colour, and somewhat easier to control, although it is perfectly acceptable to paint with the ready-prepared dyes.

When painting dye on to dry wood, the choice of timber can play a major role in the success of the project. Some timbers are much more suitable than others for this type of work. I would recommend close grain timbers such as maple, lime, hornbeam, sycamore, beech, or any of the fruitwoods. There are of course, others which are equally suitable, but it is the closeness of the grain that is so important. This physical attribute will prevent the dye from creeping along the fibres to give a fuzzy outline to the defined areas of colour. Very pretty results can be obtained by using exotic timber such as buttery piquia amerello and satinwood, especially when their delicate colours are painted with dark contrasting lines of dye.

Because the dye is to be applied to a dry surface, it will not spread, but will be absorbed into the fibres exactly where the brush has placed it. Overlap marks and brush joining lines are not desirable so this technique is really only suitable for small areas of colour, delicate designs, and patterns. In some cases, the timber can be used as a medium upon which to paint a picture, recognition of the timber still being possible through the transparent dye. However, you may be surprised how colour can confuse the eye, making timber recognition quite a puzzle.

Before painting the surface of the prepared piece, clean it with a tack cloth to remove all dust particles. When painting a piece of spindlework or end grain turning, it is possible to leave it mounted on the lathe, but for faceplate

Fig 11.1
Begin by sketching your design, then transfer it to the wood by drawing in lightly in pencil. Here you can see the preliminary sketches for this finished piece. Remember to always use a close-grained wood for this type of work – this platter was made from sycamore.

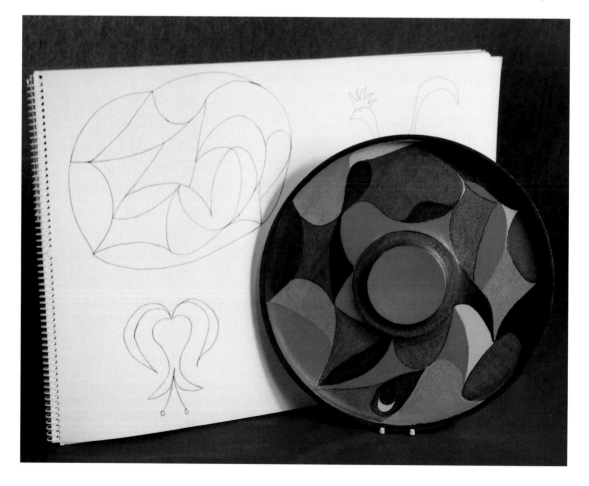

work, such as platters, you will find it much easier to take the work off the lathe and stand or sit to work on it at a convenient height. As previously suggested, a small turntable on a bench can be very helpful.

Both water and spirit dyes are suitable for painting on dry wood. For delicate painting, I use artist's pencils – that is, pointed brushes – in varying sizes. Remember to decant your selection of colours, however many you are using, but only in small quantities.

The design you choose could be a flower, abstract shapes or geometric patterns, and may require the use of several colours in clearly defined areas. Use a sketch pad to try out ideas for a design, and once you have decided on the final version, pencil it in very lightly on the turned piece (see Fig 11.1). It is important to be light of touch here, as you do not want the pencil outlines to remain visible on the finished piece.

Apply the lighter coloured dyes first, one at a time, allowing the first one to dry before applying the second, and so on (see Fig 11.2). The drying time is extremely important, as it prevents colours which lie side by side from merging, and guards against smudging should your hand accidentally touch the dye.

Should you want to blend very small areas of dye, paint the darker dye up to and a little over the lighter, before the lighter dye has dried. Remember to clean your brushes really well between visits to the palette for a

Fig 11.2
Apply the dyes one at a time, always allowing the first to dry before applying the second, gradually building up the pattern.

Fig 11.3
Use a pale French polish as a
sealer on your work before you
polish it. Remember to seal the
individual areas of colour one at a
time to eliminate any risk of
dragging one colour over another.

different colour. It is worth noting that if you are working on a pale timber, then medium and strong colours will show up better than light ones. Use the light colours as highlights, or alternatively let the natural wood show through your design to create a similar effect. A narrow dyed rim on a bowl or platter can provide an attractive framing effect.

Use a pale French polish as a sealer, carefully painting it over the individually coloured areas before polishing (see Fig 11.3).

Method 2

The second option is to apply dye on top of previously applied and dried dye (see Figs 11.4 and 11.5). Timberwise, the same guidelines apply here as those outlined for applying dye straight on to dry wood, on page 111. In the example (the flower platter), the dyed background of the rim was applied as a wash of diluted water-based dye, brushed over the dampened surface of the wood (see Fig 11.6). Once this coat of dye was fully dry, it was lightly rubbed back with fine steel wool, and then

114

Above left **Fig 11.4**
The rim of this flower platter was coloured using Method 2, applying dye over previously applied, dried dye. You can also see the preliminary sketches for the design.

Left **Fig 11.5**
Having sketched the design, paint a copy on to the platter as the main feature.

Below left and below **Fig 11.6**
Apply diluted water-based dye as a background wash on the rim over the dampened wood surface.

cleaned with a tack cloth. The background was then ready to receive a design of one or more contrasting colours (see Fig 11.7).

Top and above **Fig 11.7**
Once the background wash is dry,
paint the rim design over the top.

Above right **Fig 11.8**
Finish the platter with oil. Apply
the finish by hand using a brush to
ensure that no dye is pulled into
the uncoloured areas of the
surface, spoiling the piece.

Do not overload your brush with dye, or the dye may run. If it does, then the run will have to be incorporated into the pattern as it is impossible to rub it out!

When the dyeing process has been completed, the dye is dry and has been finally lightly rubbed over with fine steel wool and tack cloth, I recommend you finish this type of work with an oil. Where there are areas of uncoloured wood next to areas of strong coloured dye, apply the oil finish by hand, using a soft brush or pad of soft paper, working from the clean wood towards and over the dyed areas (see Fig 11.8). While not expecting the colours to bleed, this would ensure that even the smallest amount of dye would not be pulled over the undyed surface and spoil the piece.

You don't need to be hugely artistic to get a most

effective result using this technique for applying dye to wood. A neatly painted detail on a plain surface or a simple pattern, repeated around a border can be extremely attractive (see Fig 11.9). It is always worth taking a little time to develop your idea on paper before tackling your first piece.

The method of applying dye to a dry, previously dyed surface can also be used to considerable effect around the bottom of a vertical form or the exterior of a deep bowl. By using a darker dye than the base colour, brush strokes in the form of leaves or flames emanating from the bottom of the piece and flowing up the sides can accentuate the form and at the same time visually increase its stability (see Fig 11.10).

Above **Fig 11.9**
Tasteful colouring can lead to stunning results. A simple design and a plain-coloured rim serve to transform this lime bowl.

Left **Fig 11.10**
Here a flame motif was used to accentuate the form of this vase. The flames were painted on to the dry, yellow dyed background.

CHAPTER 12

Centrifuging

The technique of centrifuging has the effect of throwing outwards anything applied to the surface of the work. As I mentioned in Chapter 5, I don't recommend centrifuging spindlework, as 'outwards' will mean on to yourself! The effects of centrifuging are most easily seen on faceplate work. Centrifuging dye on the surfaces of platters, dishes or bowls with varying inner contours, ranging from virtually flat to very deep, will give an infinite variety of colouring effects, and these can be compounded by the addition of beads and coves of any size. The pieces can be of any diameter but, as a slower speed is required to safely revolve increasingly larger pieces, the resulting centrifugal force will be less than that created when revolving a smaller diameter piece at a higher speed. The resulting effects will therefore be slightly different. However, I have found it easier to control the results by reducing the speed from that used for the final turning stage, regardless of the size. The angles of the surface contours of the wood and the speed of revolution of the lathe can be used together to develop centrifuging dye as an artistic technique.

The same rigorous preparation of the work should be followed as for any other dyeing routine and, because we are using a water-based dye, the grain raising technique should also be applied. As usual, in order to achieve an even distribution of the dye, dampen the whole surface of the work.

For the first example I turned an ash dish of 10in (254mm) diameter. Stand facing the dish head on, not in line with the rim. Turn on the lathe and, with a full brush of dye, apply it to the centre of the dish, drawing the brush slowly away from the centre towards the rim. You won't get far before the brush runs dry, so dip again and make another pass, overlapping the somewhat feathered edge where the first pass finished. If you stop the lathe, you will now see a problem which can – and frequently does – occur with this technique. That is, the uneven spread of the dye. It does not form a round 'sun' as it appeared to be doing while the lathe was turned on. Instead, it forms an oval shape with two flattish sides (see Fig 12.1). The effect will be more apparent on

Fig 12.1
Centrifuging tends to create an oval shape with two flattish sides, especially when you are working with an open-grained wood, such as this ash dish.

Fig 12.2
To restore a round 'sun' at the centre of the work, lay a band of stronger colour, say red, over the yellow while the work is spinning.

Fig 12.3
Using a third colour (blue), overlap the second, and continue out to the rim. You can see that each colour is clearly defined at this stage.

Fig 12.4
To achieve a blended effect, overlay the yellow and red dyes (or whatever colours you have chosen) while they are both still wet. You can see here that the contour of the bowl has thrown the red dye over the blue area and the rim.

Fig 12.5
A final application of red dye helps to focus the yellow 'sun' again, and intensifies the fine stringing effect outwards, over the blue dye and the rim.

open-grained woods. The reason for this is that the centrifugal force pushes the dye easily along the side grain, but fails to send it across the end grain at the same speed. Because the end grain cannot soak up the dye sufficiently quickly, the side grain takes on even more, and so invariably the result is an oval 'sun'. Do not despair! There are ways to limit this strange effect.

Turn on the lathe and, with a single light colour dye, cover the whole piece. Then take a clean brush filled with a different colour dye, and overlap the first light colour coat, making another band of colour (see Fig 12.2). Take another clean brush and overlap a third colour, this time taking it out to the rim (see Fig 12.3). If you like the effect, but the colours are weak, repeat the whole process before the dye is completely dry, so that the damp surface will again assist the dye to flow. As a basic technique it is better to start with lighter colours in the centre and work towards the darker colours at the perimeter.

A blended effect can be achieved by overlaying two colours one after the other, shown in Fig 12.4, using red and yellow. The excess red dye then creeps up and outwards to the rim over the dry blue dye (see Fig 12.4). With a further application of red dye, the blended area can be transformed into a definitive line and the centrifuged effect of the dye increased (see Fig 12.5).

On close-grained woods where the oval effect is less apparent you will see that the shape the dye makes will always be concentric rings. It is impossible to achieve an eccentric design or irregular application using centrifuging unless you are turning off-centre. You should plan your design and use of colour to take account of this limitation. If bands of colour are what you require, centrifuging certainly knocks spots off painting bands on stationary work. You can describe a much more accurate circle than by hand and the technique is also great fun. The whiter, close-grained woods give the clearest colour response and provide the most accurate take-up medium. When the dye on such a piece is dry it can be used as a background for further dye painting if desired, as described in Chapter 11.

Centrifuging colour on a chestnut bowl

A chestnut bowl with a wide rim illustrates a different effect gained by centrifuging dye. With the work stationary the rim was coloured with a dark blue water-based dye. The blue was then allowed to dry thoroughly before a contrasting yellow dye was used to colour the recess (see Fig 12.6).

Above left **Fig 12.6**
The rim and recess of the chestnut bowl were carefully coloured using water-based dyes while the work was stationary, and allowed to dry.

Above right **Fig 12.7**
Yellow dye was then applied to the recess of the revolving bowl, causing it to be centrifuged over the wide rim.

Right **Fig 12.8**
Here you can see how the eye of dark blue dye threaded itself randomly across the surface of the piece giving a finishing touch.

The lathe was switched on and a brushful of yellow dye drawn from the centre of the work as far as the edge of the bowl recess, but not across the rim. More than one brushful of dye may be needed to get the desired effect. When the lathe was stopped, the centrifugal force had driven the yellow dye out of the bowl recess to form starlike threads across the rim (see Fig 12.7). You can see in Fig 12.8 how a little more yellow dye and further centrifuging increases the threadlike effect.

It is important to allow the dye to dry completely before adding any extra detail. I used a small brush to deposit an eye of the dark blue in the centre of the revolving bowl. When the lathe was switched off, some of the dye had threaded itself randomly along minute crevices of open grain, producing an original and exciting effect (see Fig 12.8).

Centrifuging on a beaded surface

The mahogany platter in Fig 12.9 shows how a beaded surface can be used, not only to help define areas of different colour, but also to mark a physical boundary against and over which the dye will collect and climb to create further fascinating results. Green dye was applied first, covering the surface completely. While still damp, it was lightly overlaid with a blue dye between the beads, which threaded its way over the outer bead to the rim (see Fig 12.10).

Before the surface dried, I applied white dye to the revolving work on the inside of the inner bead. The centrifuging carried it over the bead and the threads spread as they reached the damp flat area between the beads.

I also applied white acrylic (water-based) stain to the centre of the revolving work before it dried, drawing the brush outwards from the centre, making a sun. The centrifugal force drove the excess dye into slender threads over the dry green area (see Fig 12.11).

Although sanding sealer and wax polish will provide a

Right **Fig 12.9**
The mahogany platter with a beaded surface ready for centrifuging.

Far right **Fig 12.10**
After an all over coating of green dye, applied to the revolving work to obtain quick and even coverage, blue dye was applied over part of the damp green surface and threaded out to the rim.

Above **Fig 12.11**
Finally, white acrylic water-based stain was applied to the centre of the revolving work producing this effect.

perfectly good finish, when using close-grained woods for platters of any size, I recommend using an oil finish. It is much easier to get an even take up of oil over the changing direction of grain than it is to get an even take up of sealer. Always apply the oil while the work is stationary. To give a lovely sheen and pleasingly tactile surface, apply wax polish over the dried oil.

CHAPTER 13

Airbrushing and stencilling

Freehand airbrushing

When airbrushing, it is only possible to apply one colour at a time through a fine nozzle, so patience is required. The pot of colour attached to the airbrush is small, and will either need frequent refilling or exchanging for another bottle of the same or a different colour. Cleaning the bottle between colours is quite fiddly and inclined to be a messy job since the dye is not only in the bottle but also in the spraying mechanism itself, which needs to be thoroughly rinsed through before starting on a different colour. You really need one bottle per colour of dye if you intend to use more than one colour on any project (see Fig 13.1).

Fig 13.1
Airbrush pots frequently need refilling. The easiest solution is to have a separate pot for each colour.

Make sure that you have a large enough space in which to work, and lay out newspaper to protect other surfaces. Wear a mask fitted with a filter, to prevent inhaling the fine spray. Always make a dummy run before approaching the piece to be coloured. Try out the range of flow from the airbrush so that you are fully in control of the application. The spray can be varied from the finest mist to a pen-point delivery that you can paint with. The finest spray setting means that you can shade your work with infinite degrees of depth and light, and these areas can then be enhanced by overlaying with a second and even a third colour dye.

When spraying a single colour over a large area (say the bottom of a bowl), watch the surface carefully for signs of shine. Once a shine appears, stop spraying that area, as this is a sign that the water is sitting on the surface of the wood and is about to run. Move to another area while the wood absorbs the dye. Always take care when airbrushing in terms of the amount of dye you apply. Too much dye will result in the excess simply remaining on the surface of the work when dry, creating an unpleasant coloured haze when rubbed back.

Don't forget to allow dyes to dry between applications if you wish to describe clearly delineated areas of dye over a base colour. Spraying a second colour over a damp first coat will result in a merging of the colours. It is a good idea to practise on largish pieces of flat work first, say, three-ply, hardboard or blockboard, in order to gain confidence before approaching small pieces of turnery. I find platters and bowls the best subjects for the airbrush.

Establish an idea in your mind about your intended design or approach before starting. For example, you may want to suggest a mood, by using one or two colours, overlaid in some areas and applied with different intensities on different areas of the platter. As you select your colour and airbrush it on to your work, keep a firm hold of what you have in mind. You will find that you then transpose your thoughts along with the dye on to your work and achieve the unique expression which gives your piece individuality. Try it! The more attempts you make in this area the more effective and successful you will be.

Airbrushing a shallow bowl

Let's see how it's done. Turn the inside of a shallow bowl or dish and prepare it thoroughly for dyeing. The bowl can be left mounted on the lathe for airbrushing, which has the advantage of holding it in an upright position facing the delivery nozzle of the airbrush at 90°. Unplug the lathe and, if you wish, cover it carefully to protect it from dye spray.

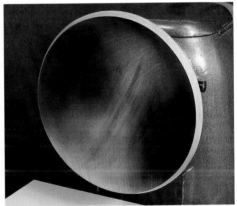

Above left and above **Fig 13.2**
The intensity of the application with an airbrush is controlled by the distance the brush is held from the work. This flexibility allows you to spray just a hint of colour, or a high intensity of colour, as shown here with blue sprayed on to a shallow sycamore bowl.

Left **Fig 13.3**
An overlaid colour effect produced by airbrushing.

Because of the fineness of the spray, it is unnecessary to dampen the surface of the work. The build up of the dye colour is easily controllable by bringing the nozzle near to the work for a more intense application, or drawing it further away for a lighter coverage (see Fig 13.2). Using this technique it is quite easy to get an impressive variation of intensity either with one colour dye or by overlaying contrasting colours (see Fig 13.3). You could also try masking over large sections of the surface in turn, using different colour dyes to overlay in the form of fine speckles, stripes, and so on. A pen point delivery can then be used to add small detail in the form of spots, line drawings or lettering.

Stencilling

The airbrushing technique can be extended to include stencilling on turned wood. The best effects can be obtained by using close-grained timber, enabling you to achieve a really crisp outline to your design.

To demonstrate this technique, I prepared a 12in (305mm) diameter sycamore platter and designed a cockerel stencil to decorate the centre, using stencils of the bird's footprints to decorate the rim.

Using one design, two effects can be created – a positive and a negative image. A positive image is achieved by spraying within the stencil, and a negative image by spraying around the outside edge of a solid shape (in this case, the cut-out of the cockerel removed to make the stencil for the positive image).

The first step is to trace your original drawings on to self-adhesive film (available from artists' supply shops) and cut out the shapes very carefully using a scalpel. Your choice of shapes could be anything, from specific to abstract (see Fig 13.4).

Remove the backing paper and carefully apply the self-adhesive stencil (positive, negative, or both) to the work (see Fig 13.5). Make sure it is thoroughly adhered, so that

Left **Fig 13.4**
Stencilling. Trace and cut out your desired image – in this case, a cockerel – from self-adhesive, paper-backed film.

Below **Fig 13.5**
The positive form of the cockerel about to be adhered to a similar shaped area of grain. I shall position it before peeling off the self-adhesive backing paper.

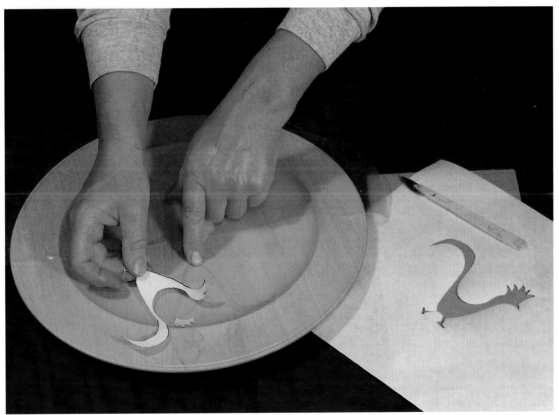

no dye will be able to creep underneath its edges and spoil the image. Now airbrush, allow the water-based dye to dry completely, and then remove the self-adhesive stencil (see Figs 13.6, 13.7 and 13.8). It is essential that the dye is fully dry before you do this, otherwise you will spoil the

Above left **Fig 13.6**
Water-based dye has been
airbrushed over the stencils.

Above centre **Fig 13.7**
When the dye has dried, carefully
peel away the self-adhesive film.

Above right **Fig 13.8**
The images of the cockerel and its
footprints can be seen clearly in
negative form.

Right and opposite **Fig 13.9**
Airbrushing the same image in
positive form, to give a symmetry
to the piece.

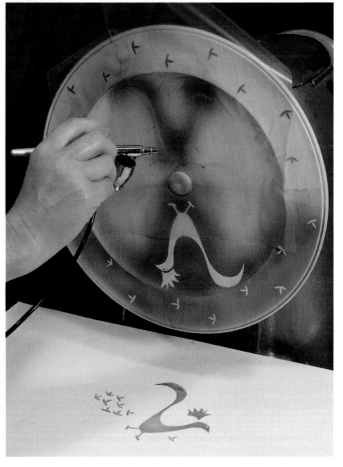

outlines of the image. Stencil the reverse (negative) image on to the work using the same techniques (see Fig 13.9).

The stencilling technique offers many possibilities for decorating and enlivening plain or coloured wood. The best finish for such pieces is oil brushed over the work to seal in the dye before polishing.

CHAPTER 14

Liming

It is possible to achieve some remarkable colour effects on turned wood beyond those produced by the straight application of dyes and stains. These effects involve the use of coloured grain fillers applied either on the natural wood or together with dyeing or staining. Black and white can be used to vary other colours, or in isolation. The following chapters cover five such 'special effects', beginning with liming.

A brief history of liming

Primarily, wood is limed in order to give it a bleached effect. But techniques and fashions change, and have been adapted to suit current requirements. In the UK, oak is synonymous with liming, not only because of its open grain structure which provides an excellent depth and variety of grain in which the lime can sit, but also because it is an indigenous timber, readily available and ideally suited to furniture making, building work and interiors, such as panelling.

Liming has been going in and out of fashion for many, many years. The two most recent resurgences of interest occurred at the turn of the century, and during the 1920s and 1930s. In the 1990s, it once again became popular, showing that rarely is anything entirely new.

Many people are now choosing to install limed oak kitchens. Oak panelling in the halls and stairways of old properties and oak bedroom furniture is being stripped and dewaxed so that it can be limed. Liming certainly gives life to oak and can lighten what some might regard as an oppressive environment. Newly cut oak for modern furniture and turned work can be a delight to the eye when limed.

Other woods for liming

There are also several exotic woods which look particularly good when limed, including wenge, padauk, bubinga, and some rosewoods, which are coarse grained with a great deal of natural colour.

Liming wax

Liming wax is a modern development which is easy to handle, gives excellent results and is prepared ready for use. The wax contains titanium oxide (a fine inorganic white pigment), solvents and wax polish. It would obviously be possible to mix your own, but for your first experiments, it is probably much easier to purchase a tin, knowing that you are using a tried and tested product.

Turning

An oak candleholder is a delightful item on which to try liming (see Fig 14.1). Choose a sound piece of oak approximately 9in (229mm) long by 3in (76mm) square. Mount it on the lathe between centres using a ring centre drive and revolving tailstock. Turn the blank to the greatest diameter cylinder possible and face off the tailstock end with a skew chisel. If it is not perfectly flat then cut it slightly concave and take it off the lathe to check that it stands without rocking before sanding it, sealing it with sanding sealer, rubbing back with fine steel wool and polishing with clear or neutral wax polish (see Fig 14.2). This completes the bottom of the candleholder. Turn the piece end for

Fig 14.1
The finished limed oak candle-holder.

Project
Oak
candleholder

Above **Fig 14.2**
Polishing the slightly concave bottom of the candleholder using a brush to apply the polish to the wood.

Above right **Fig 14.3**
Jacobs chuck and sawtooth bit. The tool rest acts as a safety barrier in front of the chuck, just in case it should come loose when revolving.

end and face off the other end. Remove the cylinder from the lathe and with a ⅞in (22mm) sawtooth bit mounted in a pillar drill, at slow speed, drill a hole in the centre of the unpolished end approximately ⅝in (16mm) deep, for the candle.

If you don't have a pillar drill it is quite easy to simulate one! Fit a Jacobs chuck into the headstock of your lathe together with the sawtooth bit (see Fig 14.3). Before turning on the lathe at its slowest speed for drilling, bring up the tool rest to a 90° angle just in front of the body of the chuck. This is purely a safety precaution lest the Jacobs chuck relinquishes its relationship with the headstock.

Locate the revolving centre in the centre mark in the bottom of the candleholder and bring up the tailstock until the point of the stationary sawtooth bit locates in the centre pin mark of the cylinder. Tighten up the tailstock and switch on the lathe. Holding the cylinder with your left hand, wind up the tailstock with your right hand, producing an accurate horizontal pillar drill (see Fig 14.4). Drill a little at a time until the required depth is reached. Withdraw the cylinder off the sawtooth bit before switching off the lathe. Remount the cylinder between the ring centre in the headstock and a small-nosed revolving centre which will fit inside the drilled candle recess (see Fig 14.5).

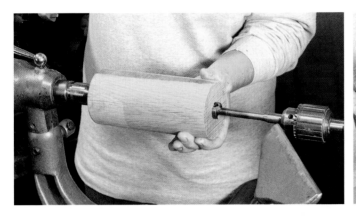

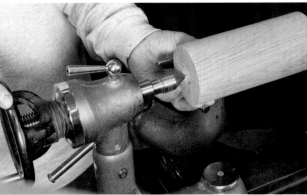

The shape for the candleholder I designed was a personal choice, and can of course be adapted. However, I kept the main body a clean, unfussy line, and cut a V detail near the base to be filled with liming wax and provide a visually stabilising feature (see Fig 14.6).

Finish the candleholder with fine abrasive and steel wool and, of course, follow the grain raising technique as a matter of course, just to improve the finish, even though the piece is not going to be dyed.

The next step is to seal the surface using a sanding sealer. I frequently use a small brush for awkward areas and a pad of paper to get an even coverage over the larger

Above left **Fig 14.4**
Holding the cylinder with your left hand, slowly wind up the tailstock. The slowly revolving sawtooth bit will drill out the hole for the candle.

Above **Fig 14.5**
The cylinder is remounted between the ring centre in the headstock and a small-nosed revolving centre which fits inside the drilled candle recess.

Below **Fig 14.6**
The simplicity of the design is enhanced but not cluttered by this V detail near the base, which will be filled with liming wax and provide an extra feature.

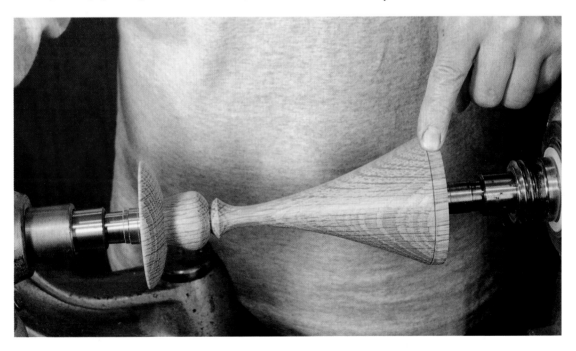

Fig 14.7
After careful preparation, seal the surface of the work with sanding sealer.

areas (see Fig 14.7). This coat will seal the surface, leaving the open grain free to be filled with the white wax.

When the sealing coat is thoroughly dry, rub back lightly with fine steel wool and wipe with a tack cloth. The latter is most important as any small particles of steel wool caught in the grain could discolour the white liming wax.

Liming

With a pad of soft paper, apply liming wax to the stationary work (see Fig 14.8). I use a circular motion so that the wax is travelling across the grain and will be sure to fill it. Make sure that the V detail is also filled. Wipe away the obvious excess with clean paper and leave it to set for 10 minutes (see Fig 14.9). Note that the wax will take longer to set in a warm temperature. Should you be interrupted at this point it is good to know that nothing detrimental will occur to the wax or the piece during your absence.

To remove the surplus set liming wax, start at one end of the revolving piece and, taking a small amount of clear wax polish on a piece of soft paper, make a short pass along the work for about 1in (25mm) or so, then change to a clean area of the paper and with a little more polish make a further pass in the same direction (see Fig 14.10). Continue in this manner until you have completed the length of the piece, then give it a final buffing with a clean cloth (see Fig 14.11).

Fig 14.8
Apply liming wax to the work
using soft paper.

Fig 14.9
Wipe away the obvious excess
wax and leave to set.

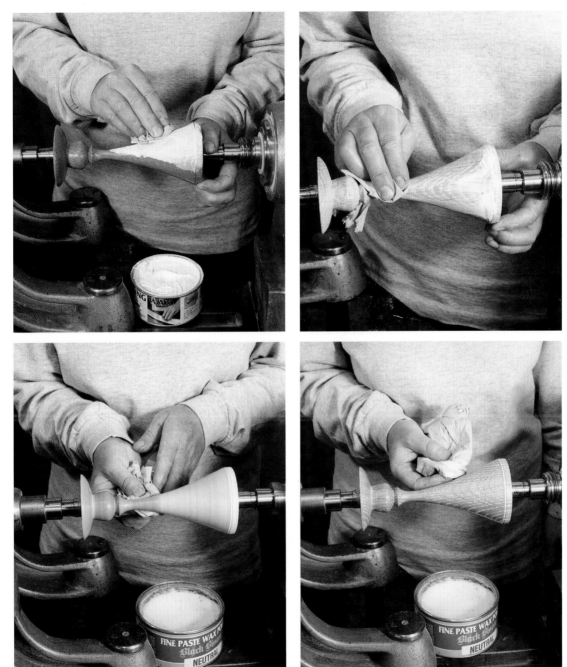

Fig 14.10
Remove excess liming wax using
clear or neutral wax polish on the
revolving work.

Fig 14.11
Buff the waxed surface to a
beautiful sheen.

Above **Fig 14.12**
A range of candleholders and lamp stands coloured with yellow and blue acrylic stain and limed.

Right **Fig 14.13**
An ash pedestal fruit bowl and vase coloured with water-based dye and limed.

Liming over colour

Colour under a lime finish gives extra contrast and an added dimension to the work. Limed ebonised timber produces extremely eye-catching effects. Dark blue and deep red together with lime are wonderfully vibrant and effective. The darker the colour, the greater the contrast; hence, deep colours are the most dramatic, and lighter colours give a more subtle effect (see Figs 14.12 and 14.13).

Woods for colouring and liming

There are several timbers suitable for colouring and liming including sweet chestnut, oak and ash which have suitable open-grain structures. Of the imported timbers, meranti, mahogany, lauan, and iroko give good results.

Turning

A piece of ash 4in (102mm) square by 12in (305mm) long will make a beautiful table lamp when turned, coloured and limed (see Fig 14.14).

Mount the blank between centres and turn to the largest diameter possible, facing off both ends, preparing one face completely. To drill the hole through which the electric wire will pass, you will need a long-hole boring kit comprising a ⁵⁄₁₆in (8mm) internal diameter hollow cup centre and pin, a counterbore (which is like a four prong drive

Project
Table lamp

Fig 14.14
The finished table lamp, coloured and limed.

Right **Fig 14.15**
The long hole boring kit. Left to right: hollow centre, shell auger, four prong counterbore. You can see the centre pin on the lathe bed.

Below **Fig 14.16**
Use a 1in (25mm) sawtooth bit to drill the hole to accommodate the counterbore.

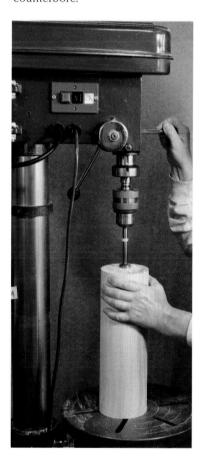

with a blunt end extended centre pin) and a ⁵⁄₁₆in (8mm) shell auger in the region of 30in (762mm) long (see Fig 14.15). Other sizes are available but ⁵⁄₁₆in (8mm) conveniently accommodates the switch fitting for the lamp.

Drill a ¾in (19mm) deep hole in the prepared end of the blank to accommodate the 1in (25mm) diameter body of the counterbore and, in the centre of this, drill a deeper ⁵⁄₁₆in (8mm) diameter hole to engage the centre pin (see Fig 14.16). The hole needs to be at least ½in (13mm) longer than the pin.

With the counterbore in the headstock, locate the drilled blank on to it and bring up the tailstock with the hollow cup centre and pin, making sure that it is centred on the original pin mark. Tighten the tailstock and spin the work briefly. Release the tailstock and you will see the ring mark the cup centre has made. Remove the pin from the cup centre and remount the blank, locating the same ring mark.

Make sure that you have engaged the slowest possible speed, and insert the long shell auger through the hollow tailstock to begin drilling (see Fig 14.17). Drill only ½ to 1in (13 to 25mm) lengths at a time, withdrawing the drill to release the spoil. If you don't pay attention to this the auger will jam. By drilling gently, you

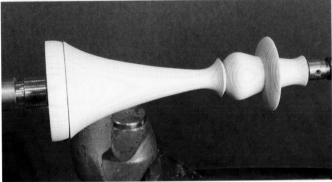

Fig 14.17
Insert the long shell auger through
the hollow tailstock to begin drilling.

Fig 14.18
The blank designed and turned.

will feel when the drill breaks through into the space
ahead of the centre pin of the counterbore.

The final preparation before shaping the lamp is to
drill a ⁵⁄₁₆in (8mm) hole from the outside edge at 90° to
the centre hole and about ¼in (6mm) up from the base,
so that the electric wire will be guided neatly away. This
can be done while the blank is mounted on the lathe, or
at the pillar drill.

Remount the cylinder and consider your table lamp
design; mine echoes that of the candleholder (see Fig
14.18). Whatever shape you choose to make, remember
to take into account stability, balance and a reasonable
simplicity of profile to do justice to the final effect
created by colouring and liming.

Complete the preparation of the piece and then follow
the procedure for applying a single colour water-based
dye (see Fig 14.19 and Chapter 8). Allow the colour to
dry thoroughly, and then use a pad of paper to apply a
coat of pale French polish over the colour while the work

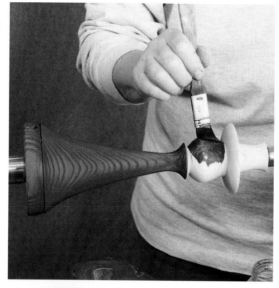

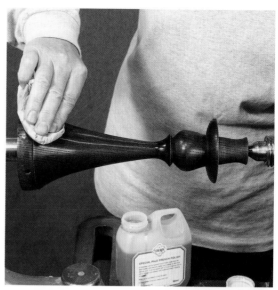

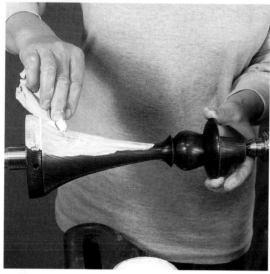

Top left **Fig 14.19**
Applying single colour water-based dye.

Top right **Fig 14.20**
Sealing with a coat of pale French polish. Sanding sealer is an alternative.

Above left **Fig 14.21**
Once the sealer or polish is dry, apply the liming wax, using a soft cloth and rubbing the wax in with a circular movement to fill the grain.

Above right **Fig 14.22**
Wipe away the obvious surplus wax.

is stationary (see Fig 14.20). Work quickly and be sure to get a good even coverage of the piece.

When the sealer is dry, apply a coat of liming wax (see Fig 14.21). With soft paper and a circular movement, fill the grain with wax. This will look an even worse mess than it did on the natural wood, but take heart, all will be well. Wipe away the obvious surplus and dispense with your 'putting on' paper (see Fig 14.22). Give the liming wax time to set hard (once again, about 10 minutes). The remaining surplus wax can now be removed using the procedures described for the candleholder.

An alternative way to remove the surplus liming wax is to use Finishing, or Danish oil instead of the wax polish, again using a little at a time on a clean area of cloth or paper for each short pass along the work (see Fig 14.23). Leave the oiled surface to dry for several hours, then give a finishing coat of neutral wax polish and buff off. In this context, the oil is only being used as an aid to easy removal of the wax and not as part of a finish. The amount of oil is minimal and so will neither add to nor detract from the sealer and wax polish finish.

Should you prefer an oiled finish which will be waterproof and stainproof, follow the slightly different procedure described for the stool project using acrylic water-based stain (see Chapter 8, page 83).

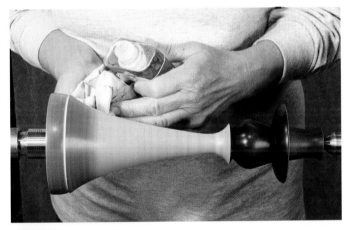

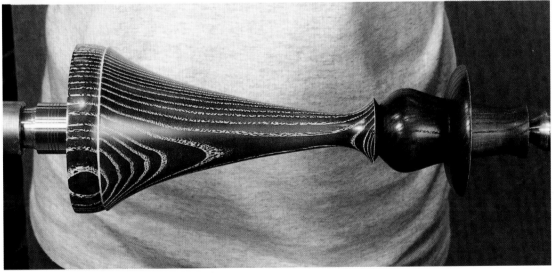

Left and below **Fig 14.23**
Remove the surplus liming wax, then polish and buff the work to a fine finish.

CHAPTER 15

Bleaching

The dictionary definition of bleaching is a process of whitening by washing and exposure (or by chemical means). Chemical bleaching removes natural colour and naturally occurring stains from wood as well as man-made stains. For the majority of woodturners using mainly new timber, uniform bleaching of the piece is more often what is required, rather than stain removal which is more frequently the lot of the furniture restorer or cabinetmaker.

As ever, the preparation of the piece is of paramount importance. Pay particular attention to following the grain rising technique very thoroughly before bleaching, as the depth of the bleaching process is not particularly great, so any form of abrading after bleaching should be minimal.

Bleaching will not prevent the natural mellowing of wood, (though it will certainly slow the process down), so don't expect the freshly bleached appearance to last for ever. An ultra-violet absorber spray will help to further guard against oxidisation.

Be sure to adhere to the necessary safety precautions when launching into any kind of chemical bleaching. Wear protective clothing and rubber gloves for mixing the chemicals and for the actual application, but *never* turn on the lathe while you are still wearing them. A moment's distraction may cause you to touch the revolving work which will grab the gloves, ripping them off in a flash. Wear a face mask or goggles, and a cartridge respirator. Have plenty of clean water available so that you can immediately wash off any accidental splashes before they have time to do any damage.

There are proprietary brands of wood bleach on the market, which come ready to use, complete with instructions, and are very effective. These solutions may not be as concentrated – and are therefore less effective – than using the chemicals in isolation, but are safer and easier to use. A repeat application may sometimes be required to achieve the desired effect.

Decant the wood bleach into a suitable container (see Fig 15.1). Working with the turned item on a flat surface will ensure greatest control over the liquid bleach especially if using it on defined areas, as is the case here.

Fig 15.1
Decant the bleach into a suitable container.

Apply the bleach solution liberally with a suitable brush, working methodically across the piece (see Fig 15.2). For small items or when using a greater volume of bleach, the article can be dipped or immersed momentarily in the liquid, but I don't recommend leaving it to soak because deep penetration of bleach increases the difficulty of neutralising it.

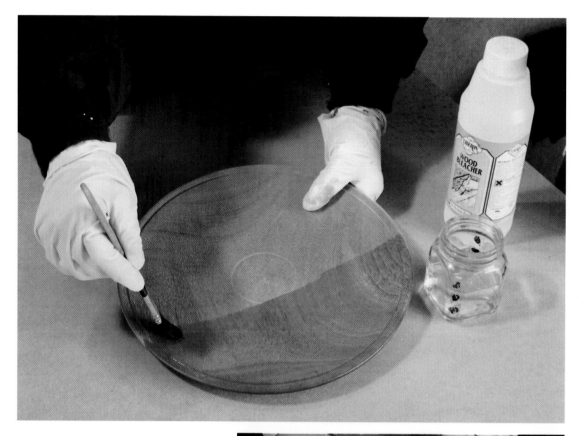

Above **Fig 15.2**
Apply the solution liberally with a brush, working methodically across the piece.

Right **Fig 15.3**
It is easy to see the chemical reaction caused by bleaching.

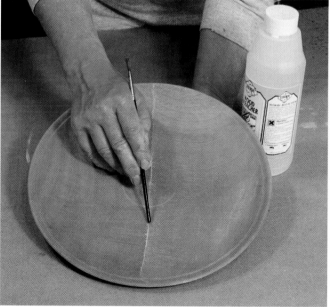

Immersion in bleach for any length of time can also result in warping, particularly in thin-walled pieces. Another effect of over-soaking can be the continuous leaching of white, powdery crystals on to the wood's surface.

This white substance which, in any case, forms on the surface of the wood as a result of bleaching, is caused by a chemical reaction, and must be washed off the work with plenty of clean water (see Fig 15.3). The piece should then be left to dry thoroughly for at least 24 hours (see Fig 15.4). If you have used an immersion method, this operation will be quite successful as long as the piece has not been immersed in bleach too long, and you should experience no subsequent leaching problems.

Dry the piece out in an airy, reasonably dry environment. Excessive humidity can result in mould forming on the wood, and too much heat can cause warping. Hopefully you will be able to use your workshop for this process, and (unless you immersed the piece) you may be able to leave the work on the lathe throughout. The before and after effects of the bleaching can clearly be seen in Fig 15.5.

Below left **Fig 15.4**
Wash off the bleach with clean water and leave the work to dry thoroughly.

Below **Fig 15.5**
The before and after effects of using a wood bleach are clearly visible here.

Once drying is complete, rub back any raised fibres using fine steel wool or very fine abrasive paper. Your choice in this will depend on the type of timber used and its reaction to the bleaching process. Be very careful not to introduce concentric sanding marks on to the work or a grey colour from the steel wool. If you feel there is a danger of this, then sand by hand in the direction of the grain with the lathe switched off.

Now clean the surface using a tack cloth, and then seal it with white polish applied with a pad of soft paper when the work is stationary. This will help to maintain the bleached effect without adding a yellow tinge.

When thoroughly dry, rub back again, and clean off the surface before applying a finishing coat of neutral wax polish.

Bleached effect

If you do not wish to attempt actual chemical bleaching, it is possible to feign a very pleasing bleached effect by adding colour to the wood. This is a very easily obtained

Fig 15.6
An ash vase 8in (203mm) high, white stained and then limed.

Fig 15.7
A mahogany platter 12in (305mm)
in diameter, which has been lightly
stained white, and then limed.

finish, for which I use white stain and liming wax, which
together give a bleached look to the work and can be
applied to any turned form (see Figs 15.6 and 15.7).

For the best results, use timber which has a regular
open grain: one of the mahogany family will be very
suitable. Prepare your turned article to perfection. I
recommend using the white acrylic water-based stain
applied to a dampened surface (see Fig 15.8). One coat
will be sufficient, but ensure that all the excess is
removed (see Fig 15.9). When it is dry, rub over with a
pad of soft paper, *not* fine steel wool, which could cause
discoloration. Then wipe with a tack cloth and seal with
a coat of white polish which will not add any unwanted
tint to the white dye (see Fig 15.10). Once the white
polish is dry, rub over again with a pad of soft paper or

Fig 15.8
Applying acrylic water-based stain to the platter, working methodically across the surface and finishing round the rim.

Fig 15.9
Using a clean sponge applicator to remove excess stain.

Fig 15.10
Sealing the work with white polish.

Fig 15.11
Filling the open grain with liming wax.

safety cloth and then fill the open grain with liming wax (see Fig 15.11).

When set, remove the surplus liming wax with neutral or transparent wax polish, a little at a time as it revolves on the lathe, working outwards from the centre (see Fig 15.12). Polish off with a safety cloth. Don't handle until the wax polish has had time to harden, to prevent finger marks from setting in the polished surface and dulling the effect.

Fig 15.12
Finally, the surplus liming wax is removed from the revolving work using a neutral wax polish.

CHAPTER 16

Patinating

Fig 16.1
An 'antiqued' elm platter 16in (406mm) in diameter, stained with mahogany colour and the rim stained black and patinated. Piece turned by John Sanders.

Patina is the sheen or lustre which pieces develop with age and use, and has an indefinable quality which adds so greatly to their value. It may derive from an accumulated film of wax and grime, built up through much handling and polishing of the item, or be simply the sheen that develops on bare wood from constant handling: old tool handles are a good example. Because patina is seen at its most appealing on really old pieces (most especially antiques), its presence, in itself, conveys a sense of age. A patinating technique may therefore be regarded as a way of creating instant age!

All woods mellow and darken with age. This is mainly caused by oxidation from sunlight, but dampness can also play its part. Both these factors are graphically illustrated by the weathered boards on garden seats and palings; even indoor furniture is affected.

A black wax known as patinating wax has been developed for use as a grain filler, and is frequently used over wood colour dyes to simulate greater age. This technique is especially useful in stool or chair making, or on smaller items, for example, bowls, platters, mirrors and lamps where such pieces are designed to fit into a historical context or used alongside antique furnishings (see Fig 16.1).

Project Bottle coaster

Fig 16.2
Having faced off the bottom of the blank, check it is flat using a rule.

The technique of patinating over wood colour dyes is very effective. Try making an antiqued bottle coaster, using a 5½in (140mm) diameter blank, 1in (25mm) deep, cut from a board of oak, chestnut, ash, mahogany or elm. Mark the centre and drill a suitable size hole for mounting on a screw chuck. Face off the bottom of the coaster, checking with a straight edge to make sure it will stand flat on a surface (see Fig 16.2).

With a pair of dividers, measure the interior diameter of a 1¾in (44mm) expanding collet chuck. Mark the bottom of the coaster, resting one side of the dividers on the tool rest and allowing only this to mark the wood. Judge by eye where the mark would match the one made by the other point of the dividers. Do not allow it to actually touch the wood or disaster will strike!

Top **Fig 16.3**
Check the collet for fit.

Top right **Fig 16.4**
Apply your chosen wood colour
dye evenly to the dampened
surface of the work.

Above **Fig 16.5**
Allow the work to dry, and seal
with sanding sealer.

Above right **Fig 16.6**
Having rubbed back with steel
wool and cleaned with the tack
cloth in the usual way, fill the
grain with patinating wax.

Use a skew chisel and a shallow fluted gouge to make
a recess ⅛in (3mm) deep on the inside of the scribed
circle. Check the collet for fit (see Fig 16.3). Finish
sanding the base, raise and flatten the grain. Then,
selecting a wood colour dye of your choice, apply it
evenly to the dampened surface (see Fig 16.4). Allow to
dry thoroughly before sealing (see Fig 16.5). Rub back
with fine steel wool and clean off with the tack cloth
before filling the grain with patinating wax (see Fig 16.6).
When set, remove the surplus wax with short passes of
soft paper using clear wax polish, or one of the wood
shades of wax polish which will body up the colour of

the dyed wood (see Fig 16.7). When all surplus is removed buff to a shine with a safety cloth (see Fig 16.8).

Now reverse the coaster on to the collet chuck and with the dividers mark a circle 3⅜in (86mm) diameter which will accommodate a wine bottle (see Fig 16.9). Use a

Above left **Fig 16.7**
I used a 'wood shade' wax polish to remove the surplus patinating wax and body up the colour of the dyed wood.

Above **Fig 16.8**
Buff to a shine with a safety cloth.

Left **Fig 16.9**
Reverse the coaster and use dividers to mark a circle large enough to accommodate the base of a wine bottle (3⅜in (86mm) is about right).

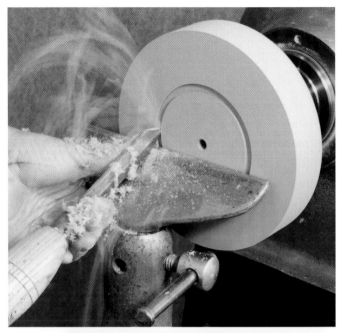

Right **Fig 16.10**
Use a parting tool to incise a cut on the inside of the marked circle.

Below **Fig 16.11**
The turned recess completed, with a decorative V in the bottom.

Below right **Fig 16.12**
There are a wide range of possible designs for the outside of the coaster: I turned a bead around the edge of the recess, followed by a V and a single sweep to the bottom beaded edge.

parting tool to incise a cut on the inside of this line (see Fig 16.10). Then, using the parting tool followed by a small deep fluted gouge, turn a vertical sided, flat bottomed recess in which the wine bottle can stand (see Fig 16.11).

A small diameter decorative V in the bottom provides a nice detail. I made a user-friendly beaded edge to the recess, followed by a V and then a single sweep towards the bottom edge, finishing with another small V and bead on the outer rim (see Fig 16.12). Of course, this design can vary greatly and it is up to the individual turner to create his or her own.

Finish preparation of the coaster with abrasives and fine steel wool. Follow the grain raising technique once more. If mahogany is used, particular attention will be needed to finishing and grain raising to achieve a satisfactory result. Apply dye, sealer, patinating wax, and finish in the same way as the underside of the coaster (see Fig 16.13). You will now have created an apparently aged piece of work, fresh off the lathe!

You will notice that at no stage do I recommend applying patinating wax straight on to the wood in the way liming wax is applied. This is because I find the black wax so searching and tenacious that it is best always to seal the wood first.

Let us now consider the possibilities of incorporating patinating on plain wood and also over a spectrum colour.

Fig 16.13
Finally, apply dye, followed by sealer and patinating wax, remove the excess wax and polish to a finish.

Project
Patinated
dish

Fig 16.14
The finished piece, turned in sweet
chestnut, 8in (203mm) in
diameter, coloured and patinated.

A piece of open-grained sweet chestnut 8in (203mm)
diameter and 1½ or 2in (38 or 51mm) thick makes a
lovely little dish on which to display the plain patinated
and colour-patinated effects (see Fig 16.14).

Turning

Mount the blank on a screw chuck and true the outer
edge. Move the tool rest to sit across the face of the work
and level it across. Make a small 1¾in (44mm) shallow
dovetail-shaped recess for the expanding collet chuck
(see Fig 16.15). Leaving a flat shallow ¼in (6mm) wide
foot, make a long sweeping profile to the outer edge,
finishing just below the top edge.

Finish the bottom of the dish with abrasives, steel wool
and clean off with a tack cloth. As we shall not be
applying dye to the bottom of the dish it is not essential
to raise the grain.

Coat the work with sanding sealer and when totally dry rub back lightly with fine steel wool and wipe over with a tack cloth (see Fig 16.16). Then, with the work stationary, take a small amount of black patinating wax on soft paper and work it across the grain in a circular movement in order to fill the grain completely (see Fig 16.17).

It is a good idea to wear a pair of lightweight rubber gloves for this job. The black wax is very searching, and not only will it fill the grain of the wood, it will mark *everything else* it comes into contact with, so an awareness of where you put the used soft paper is also necessary!

Your work will look an awful mess when you have completely covered it with the black wax, but, as with the liming technique, do not despair. Wipe away any surplus wax, discard your gloves and the soiled paper and leave the wax to set. The setting time is only a matter of about 10 minutes but it may take a little longer in higher temperatures.

As always, be certain to remove your gloves before turning on the lathe and, with clean paper and clear wax, take a little at a time and remove the excess black wax, making short passes about ½in to 1in (13 to 25mm)

Below left **Fig 16.15**
Finishing off the dovetail recess using an oval skew chisel.

Below centre **Fig 16.16**
Coat the work with sanding sealer.

Below right **Fig 16.17**
Unplug the lathe before putting on a rubber glove to coat the piece with patinating wax, working across the grain in a circular motion using soft paper.

Above **Fig 16.18**
Using clear or neutral wax polish to clean off the piece.

Above right **Fig 16.19**
When all the surplus patinating wax has been removed, give the work a final coat of wax polish and buff. You can see the patinated effect very clearly here.

long. Start in the middle and work towards the rim (see Fig 16.18). Turn to a clean part of your cloth and repeat the procedure. When no more surplus wax comes off, give one more pass with a fresh coat of wax and then buff off with a safety cloth (see Fig 16.19). Check that the recess is free from surplus black wax before finishing.

Reverse the dish on to the expanding collet chuck, and after facing off make a rim about 2in (51mm) wide sloping from the top of the dish, down to meet the outer edge. At this stage the piece will look rather like a flying saucer! Now turn out a depression about 4in (102mm) wide and 1in (25mm) deep in the centre to form a dish. I love the wide rim and comparatively small depression in this bowl which enables us to see the colour contrast equally. The diameter of the bowl is about the same as double the width of the rim. The cut needs to be one continuous elliptical flow.

Complete preparations of the dish and follow the grain raising technique in the depression as this will be coloured with water-based dye. When the work is dry and fully prepared, carefully dampen the area to be dyed with a clean brush and clean water. Be precise with the edges – runs of water or brushing over the defined area will tempt the dye to follow suit, chasing along the wet grain (see Fig 16.20). Then apply your chosen colour of water-based dye, evenly covering the dampened area (see Fig 16.21). Allow to dry thoroughly. Rub back lightly with fine steel wool and clean the piece with the tack cloth. The whole surface can now be sealed. With soft paper to aid even coverage, methodically seal the uncoloured area first and then the coloured wood. I always follow this order so that, should a little of the dye come off on to my paper, I can be sure not to spread it on to the natural wood (see Fig 16.22).

After sealing and lightly cutting back, apply black patinating wax and follow the processes described for the underside of the bowl (see Fig 16.23). Of course, you could cut features on to your work and fill them with the patinating wax too. A simple feature like a V can improve a piece enormously. It can be used on a rimmed dish or platter to describe a frame and effectively give the eye the parameters of the piece, or of the coloured area.

Below left **Fig 16.20**
Dampening the inside of the bowl, being careful not to run over the edges.

Below right **Fig 16.21**
Apply the water-based dye precisely to the dampened area.

Bottom left **Fig 16.22**
Sealing the undyed rim before proceeding to seal the coloured area.

Bottom right **Fig 16.23**
Applying black patinating wax to the coloured and uncoloured areas, using a circular motion to ensure that the black wax fills the grain.

When set, remove the surplus wax as before to give a polished finish (see Figs 16.24, 16.25 and 16.26). I call this kind of piece a pebble dish – my inspiration was drawn from a pebble beach on which I found old weathered timbers sporting gorgeous yellow lichen.

Above **Fig 16.24**
Removing surplus wax from the revolving work with neutral wax. You can see here that I support the hand holding the cleaning paper with my free hand.

Above right **Fig 16.25**
Here you can see the surplus patinating wax transferred to the cloth from the work.

Right **Fig 16.26**
Once all the surplus wax has been removed, the piece is buffed to a fine finish using a safety cloth.

CHAPTER 17

Ebonising

I had long puzzled over the difference between ebonising and colouring something black, and felt that I was missing out on some incredibly secret and obscure process.

Ebonising simply means making something resemble ebony – that is, the black bits. The main features of ebony are its close-grain structure and the density of its fibres. These enable turners and other woodworkers to obtain extremely beautiful finishes (piano keys are a good example). The pure black colour commonly associated with the name is usually a feature of the heartwood, although some ebonies are naturally streaked with brown or with grey.

When used imaginatively and well, a blackened piece of turned wood becomes a two-dimensional profile and can be cleverly used to illustrate negative form (see Fig 17.1).

Of course, when photographing turned black objects one invariably sees a patch of light reflected on the curved surface of the work, immediately challenging the brain either to accept this two dimensional image as it is seen, or to transpose it into the three dimensional object which it actually is.

Fig 17.1
Ebonised or blackened pieces of turnery can in some senses be viewed as two-dimensional forms, allowing for the emergence of 'negative forms' between them.

Substitute the word silhouette for two-dimensional and the word ebonising for dyeing something black, and the possibilities for presentation of the artistic form immediately take on a different meaning.

Dyed sycamore, when blackened, is known as poor man's ebony, due to its similarity in grain. Sycamore readily takes up dye and, as long as it is of best quality, will give an excellent finish. If we are truly trying to emulate the best ebony and use it to promote form as a two-dimensional image, then timbers similar to sycamore, like lime, maple and beech are also suitable.

Fig 17.2
Samples of ebonised turnery in different woods. Left to right: bodo, bog oak, holly, ebony and ash.

Many other timbers will take on an excellent black colour from dye or stain, although I feel that successful ebonising can owe more to the method of colouring than to the timber itself (see Fig 17.2). It is important to remember, of course, that dye allows the grain to be seen, whereas paint is opaque and can be used successfully on wood where profile is all important and the distraction of the grain is not required. Black dyes and stains vary in their opacity; some have a tendency to brown and can be disappointing. An example of totally natural ebonising is bog oak, where the ebonising process has taken place over many centuries as the fallen trees lay immersed in the peat bogs. So if you have any bog oak offered to you, you can be sure that it will be ebonised! It is a good wood to turn but, being completely unstable when freshly dug up, it needs to dry out very slowly before turning. If not completely dry, it is capable, even in a solid mass, of turning from round to oval in section.

There are several methods of obtaining a good black colour on turned work; experiment with each to see what suits you and your project best.

Method 1

Begin by turning a piece of sycamore, holly or lime, but do make some drawings of a shape first, whether it is spindle work or end grain, solid, hollow form or box. Pay particular attention to the profile, because this is where your labours will ultimately be rewarded. The design need not be complicated; clean lines and proportion are the first requirement and, ultimately, we are looking for a piece which is bold, balanced and *black* (see Fig 17.3). Prepare the piece to perfection. As ever, this is very important when staining close-grained woods since any imperfections, by way of concentric sanding marks or torn grain will become a major source of irritation when the piece is finished.

Follow the grain raising procedure, and then lightly dampen the surface of the work, before applying a coat of black

Fig 17.3
Clean lines and proportion best complement the stunning effect of jet-black wood, as this holly vase demonstrates.

165

Above and above right **Fig 17.4**
As usual, begin with the grain raising procedure, lightly dampen the surface of the work and then apply a coat of black water-based dye, usually called simply 'ebony'.

Below **Fig 17.5**
You will find the first coat displays a brownish hue.

water-based dye, usually called 'ebony' (see Fig 17.4). Use a brush large enough to cover the surface, making bold strokes along the length of the piece. This first coat is likely to display a somewhat brownish hue (see Fig 17.5). When it shows signs of drying, apply a second coat all over. Allow this to dry thoroughly before rubbing back very lightly with fine steel wool. After the second coat of black dye, the depth of colour will have improved remarkably, but you may still be able to see a brownish tinge (see Fig 17.6). Don't despair. Throw convention to the wind and, with a clean brush, apply a coat of *spirit*-based ebony dye. You will notice at once the improvement in the quality of the colour (see Fig 17.7). Spirit dye over water dye *will* work, but remember that they *must* be applied in this order – water-based followed by spirit-based, never the other way round. Don't forget to decant the different dyes into suitable palettes.

You should now have an acceptable black finish. When it is really dry, after lightly going over with fine steel wool, reinforce the colour by applying a coat of black patinating wax, and buff it off as a final polish (see

Fig 17.8). Don't be tempted to put clear wax polish over it, as this will remove the patinating wax. If you are looking for an added effect on an ebonised piece, you might consider cutting back through the colour with a skew chisel, making a V near the bottom of a vase or above the shoulder to give a contrasting white line.

Above left **Fig 17.6**
After the second coat of dye the depth of colour will have improved, but you may still be able to see a hint of brown. You can see I am decanting some spirit-based dye in readiness for the next stage.

Above **Fig 17.7**
A vast improvement in the colour is quickly achieved by applying a coat of spirit-based dye.

Centre left and left **Fig 17.8**
The colour can then be further reinforced by an application of black patinating wax, buffed to a shine.

Method 2

If you have only a range of water-based dyes, try using dark blue as the first coat (see Fig 17.9). This undertone seems to correct any tendency to brown in the following

Fig 17.9
If you only have a range of water-based dyes available, an alternative method is to begin by giving the work a coat of dark blue.

Fig 17.10
A subsequent application of ebony water-based dye is then 'colour corrected' by the blue underneath, avoiding any brown tinge to the colour.

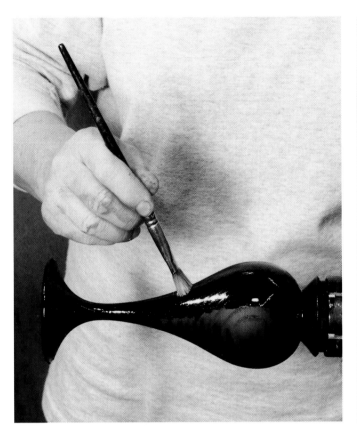

Fig 17.11
To finish off, apply two or three coats of finishing oil, and buff to a sheen when dry. Don't forget to dye the underside of the foot after parting off.

coat of ebony water-based dye (see Fig 7.10). If necessary, apply a second coat of the ebony dye before finishing. Apply two or three coats of Finishing oil and buff to a sheen when dry (see Fig 17.11).

Method 3

A third option was brought to my notice when my husband returned from the workshop with one of the numerous pieces from his expanding repertoire of Tudor-type large bowls and platters. He uses mainly badly coloured ash, elm or walnut which is old and worm-holed. However, it is ideal for wood colour stains and patinating to give an aged finish to these antique looking pieces. The piece was a beaded, open bowl which he had coated with three applications of black acrylic water-based stain, buffing up the final application to a lovely sheen on the lathe. It was very tactile and quite different from my profile approach, but the depth of colour of black was excellent, highlighting a new option for ebonising which can be applied to any turned item.

Method 4

Instead of using a ready-made dye, you can make up your own chemical stain, using white vinegar in which iron filings, steel wool or steel nails have been soaked. Try using 1oz (28g) filings to 1 pint (570ml) vinegar, straining off the liquid after 24 hours. A weak solution will turn oak a silvery grey and make sycamore a pretty grey. If the solution is strong, it will make oak black. Apply successive coats until the depth of colour is quite dark. An oil finish will bring out the stain to appear black.

Method 5

A simple and effective way of ebonising a form is by spraying it with matt cellulose car spray. Spraying from different angles will ensure an even and complete coverage (see Fig 17.12). This may sound an easy option but don't be misled. Preparation counts for everything. Spray outside on a still day and wear a mask. In the workshop protect machinery and tools from the mist. Don't overspray or runs of paint will spoil your work.

Fig 17.12
Ebonising a vase using matt black cellulose car spray. Keep the can about a foot away from the piece as you spray.

Fig 17.13
To achieve a gloss finish use a
carnauba stick and then polish up
with a soft cloth.

Always start spraying before approaching the work so that
you can check the flow. The paint is inclined to obscure
the grain but this will probably be acceptable in this
particular instance. The paint will be a finish in its own
right, but don't be tempted to handle it until it is
completely hard. Spraying from different angles will
enable you to achieve an even coverage. As with all
colouring techniques, don't forget to ebonise the
underside, or bottom of a piece. It can be a shock and will
certainly ruin the effect of a piece when someone picks
up an 'ebony' bowl or vase, and on looking at the bottom
– they always do – sees it is sycamore.

In complete contrast to the matt finish obtained with
cellulose spray, a gloss finish can be obtained by using a
carnauba stick as explained in the section on finishing (see
page 26). This is best used over a dyed surface (see Fig 17.13).

If you are experimenting or require only to colour small
areas black, such as beads or narrow rims, there are a host
of other blackening products which you can try out. They
include Indian ink and other artists' inks as well as shoe
dye. Permanent marker pens and felt-tip pens can also be
used. Although none of these items has been developed
for the woodturner, there is nothing against using them if
they do the job that is required, which can range from
experimental work to being the only item to hand when a
touch-in job is required over a bit of damage on the way
to an exhibition. Try putting as many options as possible
to the test before deciding which black is best for you.

CHAPTER 18

Gilding

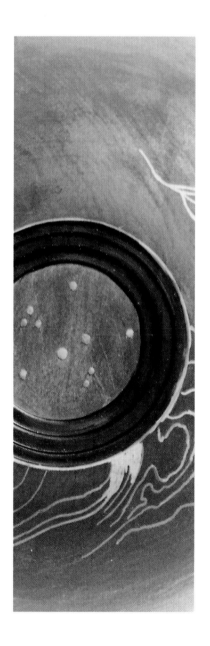

Contemporary dictionaries define the process as 'covering or overlaying with gold or any gold-like substance'. But, while the art of gilding with fine gold leaf continues today, cost has led to the use of other techniques to gain similar effects.

The ancient Egyptians were master gilders, practising their art on mummy cases and furniture. From the earliest times, the Chinese have ornamented wood in this way, as well as pottery and textiles. The Greeks gilded wood, masonry and metals, and from the Greeks the Romans acquired the art that made their temples and palaces resplendent with brilliant gilding.

Gilding also covers the application of silver, palladium, aluminium, and copper alloys. With modern technology, bronze powders are used in place of the costly powdered gold in gilding products and the colour range has been extended to include several golds, bronze, silver, pewter, and copper in a range of creams, varnishes and oil-based metallic paints.

Metal transfer leaf is a very convincing substitute for real gold leaf, and gilt filler sticks, marker pens and fibre-tip pens extend the list of available gilding products. They give the opportunity to create a wide range of lustrous effects on newly turned or flat timber, as well as being used to retouch old gilded furniture and picture frames. Gilding can be regarded as the icing on the cake – the final touch to a piece of work.

Fig 18.1
Gilding can give a piece elegance and artistic presence.

When considering a gilt finish, whatever the choice of colour, remember this is not a dye. The gilt will not be absorbed by the wood, but will sit on the surface and, in doing so, obliterate or fill the grain, depending on the product used. Gilt can embellish wood with a superlative lustre and, when selectively used, is capable of lifting a beautifully coloured piece of turned wood, giving it the artistic presence to stand alongside the magnificent forms and radiant colours which have been extended to glass and ceramics for centuries (see Fig 18.1).

Gilt varnish

Gilt varnish is available ready to use in several colours and has been extensively used for many years by picture framers, furniture restorers and artists. It can be used on new wood, and for repainting and touching up antique pieces. Only recently has it been introduced into the work of artistic woodturners.

Gilt varnish can be used to gild parts of newly turned pieces such as the rim of a platter or bowl, a complete picture frame or a detail like a bead or cove. With fine brush work, it is ideal for mark making or describing lines to define a particular area on a piece. It can be used as a highlight, or a peripheral line to emphasise a coloured shape. The extensive colour range is easily applied by brush as the viscosity makes it flow well, drying to a shiny, hardwearing finish. The spirit base causes it to be toxic and highly flammable, so it should be treated with respect. Spillages and brushes can be cleaned with white spirit.

It is essential to ensure that the liquid gilt varnish is well shaken or mixed before applying to the work with a suitable soft-haired brush. It is worth making a dry run with the brush to ensure it is neither too large nor too small for the job and is of a suitable shape for the area to be gilded. Dampen the brush with clean white spirit first so that it forms its painting profile.

The drying time is normally several hours, but always adhere to the manufacturer's instructions. I have found it wise to allow two days to ensure complete hardening.

Gilt varnish on close-grained wood

Woods like sycamore, apple, or maple are so beautifully close-grained that the gilt varnish can be brushed directly on to the prepared wood without the need for an undercoat of any kind. On a flat ½in (13mm) rim, the strokes are best made with a round-ended brush, working methodically around the circumference in one direction

Fig 18.2
Brushing gilt varnish on to the rim of a sycamore bowl using a small round-ended brush.

(see Fig 18.2). If you leave a feathered edge at the start you can then lap over it as the rim or frame is completed.

A bead is best covered by drawing the brush in short strokes first along one side and then the other in the same direction as the bead runs, filling in the centre last of all. The same technique can be used for a cove. If one application does not provide sufficient coverage, allow it to dry thoroughly before applying a second coat.

The dry second coat will give a shiny, long lasting finish and, if ever damaged, can be touched up or alternatively rubbed back with fine abrasive to a smooth surface and then recoated with the same gilt varnish colour.

Remember never to handle your work until the varnish has had sufficient time not only to dry, but also to harden.

Gilt varnish over colour

For effective mark-making or gilt line drawing on top of colour, the close-grained woods undoubtedly provide the superior surface on which to work. Colour your piece of

Fig 18.3
This 10in (254mm) diameter wall decoration was turned in sycamore and colour blended in blue, black and purple. Gilt varnish markings were then applied.

work using the water-based dyes and any of the techniques described earlier to achieve the desired effect. When the finishes have been applied, use the gilt varnish with a fine brush to describe whatever type of gilt marks or lines you have in mind (see Fig 18.3).

Gilt varnish over a fontenay base

When applying gilt varnish to open-grained wood, for instance around the rim of an ash or oak bowl or platter, it is necessary to fill the grain first, using a fontenay base, which is a spirit-based dense liquid. It has been specifically designed as a grain filler, sealer and undertone for use on open-grain woods prior to covering with gilt varnish or gilt cream.

There are several colours of fontenay from which to

choose. Black fontenay is recommended for use under silver and pewter gilts, red or yellow fontenay beneath golds, copper, and bronze (see Fig 18.4). With experience you will choose the colour that gives the undertone which pleases you most.

Be aware that fontenay is flammable and toxic. White spirit will remove it from brushes, but it will colour any areas of wood with which it comes into contact.

Before applying it to areas to be covered by the gilding, shake or mix the fontenay really well. Brush the fontenay on to the precise area to be gilded (see Fig 18.5). Work progressively in one direction along the detail of the piece. Leave a feathered end where you have

Left **Fig 18.4**
A plain ash bowl with the alternative materials required to gild it: black fontenay base and silver gilt varnish (left), together with red fontenay and a gold gilt varnish (right) and a selection of suitable brushes.

Below **Fig 18.5**
Begin by brushing the appropriate fontenay base on to the area to be gilded. For the best results, be very precise in this application.

started with the fontenay which you can lap over on completion. This will be relevant to a circular application. However, if the areas are of geometric shapes, then coat them as carefully and precisely as possible, making good edges. Vs or coves can be painted along their length cutting in with a neat upper edge. The fontenay tends to dry quite quickly, so it is sensible to cover the ground fairly rapidly. If the coverage is not as good as you intended with one coat, don't try to patch it up. If you go back to it before it dries, you will pull up the first coat, so leave it, and let it dry thoroughly. Rub back any roughness very carefully with fine abrasive and apply a second coat over the whole area.

There is a lot of difference between touch dry and thoroughly dry. Touch dry relates to the feel and look of the visible surface, and should it be abraded, even slightly, the abrasive will cut through the outer touch dry skin, and destroy the substance beneath. So try to be patient with all drying times. It can make a huge difference to the finished appearance of a piece.

A fontenay base is absolutely essential for achieving a

Below and below right **Fig 18.6**
Once the fontenay has been applied, the gilt varnish can be carefully brushed on over the top. Here you can see I have applied red fontenay and black fontenay bases to the rim of this bowl, ready to receive coats of gold and silver gilt varnish respectively.

good gilt finish on open-grained woods because gilt varnish on its own does not have the substance of a grain filler and its surface tension prevents it from filling the open grain (see Fig 18.6).

The selected fontenay colour can add an extra dimension or antique effect, if it is allowed to show through the gilt (see Fig 18.7). This is achieved by less than completely covering the fontenay base with the gilt varnish.

If you prefer a complete and thorough gilding, a

Left **Fig 18.7**
Fontenay base can add an 'antique' effect to a piece if it is allowed to show through the gilt. You can see this effect on the rim of this bowl.

Below **Fig 18.8**
Two coats of gilt varnish will give a bright and hardwearing surface, such as the rim of this bowl.

second coat of gilt varnish can be applied, but only when the first is thoroughly dry. When dry and hardened, the gilt varnish can be lightly buffed with a soft cloth and will provide a bright, hardwearing surface (see Fig 18.8).

Gilt cream

Gilt cream is a waxy cream substance supplied in the same range of colours as gilt varnish. This enables the colour gilder to use matching gilt cream and gilt varnish for different effects on the same piece of work.

Gilt cream is soft enough to be smoothed on to the wood quite easily by fingertip or a small pad of cloth, but is normally too firm to apply by brush, although its consistency varies a lot between summer and winter temperatures. It will provide a most appealing sheen finish which, although not particularly hardwearing, is perfectly satisfactory for frames, turned work and other pieces which are not going to be handled to any great extent. It gives a much softer, gentler finish than the brightness of the gilt varnish.

Gilt cream on open-grained wood

Gilt cream can be used as a finish on the flat or dished rim of a piece of turned work just as easily as a gilt varnish (see Fig 18.9). On open grained wood, apply one or two coats of the chosen colour of fontenay base first. When dried and rubbed to a smooth surface, the gilt cream can be applied a little at a time with the finger tip working in one direction, to cover the circumference of the work.

Once applied, don't go back over it to add extra cream

Fig 18.9
Gilt creams and their respective finishes on turned work. Top to bottom: gold, silver and copper.

– you will probably only succeed in disturbing the first coat. If the coverage of the first coat is not good enough, allow the cream to set, and only then apply a second covering. As with the gilt varnish, you may prefer to leave glimpses of the fontenay showing through the subtle sheen of the cream. For extra protection the cream can be covered with a coat of transparent gilt finishing liquid, a colourless varnish specially designed for the purpose.

Gilt cream as a grain filler

An exciting effect can be created by taking a lateral approach to gilding, using the gilt cream as a grain filler. This can only satisfactorily be done with the gilt cream and not the varnish.

Fig 18.10
A shallow dish turned from lauan. The setting sun effect was achieved using water-based dyes and the centrifuging technique. Gilt cream was used as a filler on the body of the piece, with a matching gilt varnish on the rim.

When applied over colour, the result provides a new element of surprise and delight, and is very exciting for the artistic woodturner, as well as the viewer. I suggest keeping this technique for special pieces. Be selective and don't be tempted to plaster it on everything you make and colour.

It can be used on the body of a piece of work in conjunction with the matching varnish around the rim. The results can be a delight to the eye (see Figs 18.10 and

Fig 18.11
You can see how gilt varnish has been used to fill the grain on this 14in (356mm) high pedestal vase, applied over blended water-based dyes.

18.11). You could choose to gild over a single colour, blended colours, grain-guided colouring, ebonising, or a combination of these techniques.

Gilt grain filler with an oiled finish

If the piece of work in question is to have an oiled finish, so that it is stainproof and waterproof, or you have selected oil because of its ease of application, then after dyeing your work, apply the gilt cream directly over the colour in the usual way, either all over the piece, or only to specific areas. When the cream has set, remove the surplus with Finishing or Danish oil.

The action of the oil is two-fold. Not only is it removing the surplus gilt cream, it is also acting as a sealer. When the excess gilt cream has been removed apply a more liberal coat over the whole surface. This will act as a sealer, and needs to soak into the wood, where it will set hard and form a waterproof barrier. Apply three progressively lighter coats of oil, making sure that each previous coat is dry, and rub back gently with the fine steel wool between coats. The final coat can be buffed gently to a sheen. If you prefer a presentation shine, apply a neutral wax polish on top, and gently buff off.

This finishing technique can be applied to spindlework too. When applying the grain filling gilding technique to spindlework on the lathe, a high gloss finish can be achieved by using a carnauba block as the polish. However, care must be taken not to create so much heat that the gilt cream is melted and removed. I do not recommend using carnauba block on bowls or platters.

Metal transfer leaf

If you wish to use something closer to gold leaf, then try metal transfer leaf, which is easier to handle than real gold leaf, and much less expensive. It is available in gold, silver and aluminium colours. The fine metal leaves are presented on wax paper backing (see Fig 18.12).

Preparation of the piece before applying leaf is all important. On open-grained wood the gilding will look best when applied over an appropriately coloured and filled base. Gesso, also known as bole, is a specially formulated plaster base for use as a sealing coat, under metal leaf. Using a small brush, paint on a coat of red or yellow gesso for use under gold transfer leaf, or blue, black or yellow for use under silver leaf, based on personal preference. When dry, the gesso finish should be very gently abraded to give as smooth a surface as possible. With close-grained woods I have found it quite satisfactory to omit the gesso application and apply the gold size to the bare wood (see Fig 18.13). However, if gesso has been applied, use a fine brush and meticulously paint a light coat of gold size over the area to be gilded.

Wait until the area is tacky then take a sheet of transfer leaf and press it leaf-side down on to the sized wood.

Below **Fig 18.12**
Metal transfer leaf, which is supplied on a wax paper backing, protected by a tissue cover over the top. Handle with care!

Below right **Fig 18.13**
Sizing the area to be gilded.

Bottom **Fig 18.14**
Press the transfer leaf leaf-side down on to the wood surface and rub down firmly with your fingers.

Bottom right **Fig 18.15**
Peel off the backing paper and any superfluous transfer leaf.

Fig 18.16
Finish by smoothing over the leaf with a cotton wool pad.

Rub it firmly down with your fingers, then peel off the wax backing paper (see Figs 18.14 and 18.15).

Continue the process over the sized area so that you complete the job before the size becomes too dry. Using the same procedure, repair any areas where the leaf may have shredded away from the surface. Finish by smoothing over the leaf with a cotton wool pad (see Fig 18.16).

Gold and silver marker pens

Marker pens contain an oil-based paint, are easy to use, and, with such a beautifully fine point, are superb for very fine line drawings and mark making, especially on close-grained woods (see Fig 18.17). They can be applied over dried spirit- or water-based dyes and washes, and can be used in conjunction with the gilt varnish in areas of work just too fine for a brush.

Fig 18.17
This ebonised 12in (305mm) diameter lauan platter is the perfect foil for decoration with a gold marker pen.

Gold and silver felt-tip pens

Felt-tip pens can be useful for creating a decorative gilt effect, although far removed from the real thing. The felt tip can be cut to any shape with a scalpel, and is useful for marking a neat edge to a gilded area, or lining out coloured work, more particularly on furniture.

Gilt filler sticks

Filler sticks are available in gold, silver, copper and bronze and can be used to fill cracks and crevices in new or damaged gilded articles. From an artistic viewpoint, they can also be used to fill intentionally created holes and crevices (see Fig 18.18). Areas of open

Fig 18.18
An 11in (279mm) diameter
sycamore bowl, showing the use
of gilt filler stick to provide added
detail over the colour, and
compliment the gold pen work.

burr and other naturally occurring blemishes, which
may not always be acceptable in their raw state, provide
intrigue to the viewer when filled with gilt. Combine
these gilt filled areas with a gilded turned detail, such as
a V or bead, and they become truly decorative.

Because there are so many options and choices to be
made when gilding, here is a project where the selection
has been made for you. This will help you to gain sufficient confidence to experiment with the alternatives.

An ash bowl blank of 10–12in (254–305mm) diameter
and 2in (51mm) thick will make a generous bowl for
mounting on a pedestal made from another piece of ash
of 4in (102mm) diameter and 5in (127mm) long.

Project
Gilded
pedestal
bowl

Turning and colouring the bowl

Make the bowl first, mounting the blank on a screw chuck or faceplate, whichever you prefer. Remember to reduce the speed of the lathe for a blank of this size.

True the blank and face off, making a 2in (51mm) diameter recess in the bottom face for remounting on the expanding collet chuck. However, because the recess is going to accommodate the pedestal, cut it no less than ⅛in (3mm) deep so that it will form a reasonable joint.

The outside shape of the bowl flows in a single sweep leaving a ¼in (6mm) flat rim surrounding the recess, and then flows smoothly to finish ¼in (6mm) below the upper edge. Sand the outside of the bowl, and carry out the grain raising procedure prior to colouring with a water-based dye or dyes. On a dampened surface these may be applied singly or blended using one, two, or more colours, as we saw in Chapters 8 and 9 (see Fig 18.19). The guide to eventual success is to remember that the gilding will contrast better with stronger colours than it will with delicate ones.

Fig 18.19
I chose to blend two water-based dyes on the underside of the bowl.

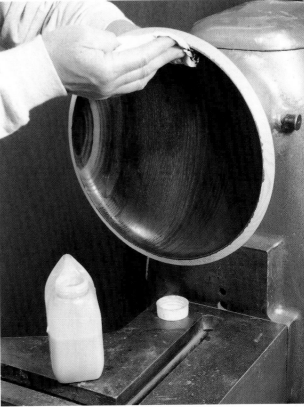

Above left **Fig 18.20**
The underside sealed and polished.

Above **Fig 18.21**
Sealing the dry interior of the
bowl after colouring.

Allow plenty of drying time, rub back gently with fine
steel wool, seal and polish (see Fig 18.20). Reverse the
bowl on to the expanding collet chuck and cut a dished
½in (13mm) wide rim, tilted upwards to the inner edge.
Turn out the bowl to about ¼in (6mm) thick, following
the profile of the outer surface. Slightly undercut the rim
and be sure the flow is continuous and does not harbour
ridges or a centre bump or pip. Complete by abrading
and following the grain raising technique. Dampen the
surface once more and apply your chosen selection of
water-based dye colours, using the grain to its best
advantage. Ignore the rim itself, but colour right up to it.
Don't worry if the dye creeps over the rim a little; this
won't matter. When finished allow to dry thoroughly and
lightly rub down with fine steel wool and tack cloth. Seal
the interior of the bowl but not the rim, with sanding
sealer on a pad of paper. Rub back when this is really dry,
and clean with a tack cloth (see Fig 18.21).

To reduce handling the gilded bowl when trying the pedestal for fit, it is a good idea to put it to one side and make the pedestal next, returning later to complete the gilding of the bowl.

Turning and colouring the pedestal

Mount the pedestal blank between centres using a ring centre drive. Turn to a cylinder. Face off the tailstock end and sand to finish (see Fig 18.22). Turn the cylinder end for end and then set a pair of callipers to the diameter of the recess in the bowl.

Right **Fig 18.22**
Facing off the ash blank for the pedestal.

Below **Fig 18.23**
With callipers as a guide, a parting tool is used to cut a spigot to fit the recess in the bowl.

Below right **Fig 18.24**
Shaping the pedestal using a small, deep fluted gouge. Note the flat surface next to the spigot.

190

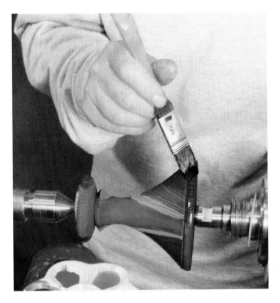

Face off the other end of the pedestal and cut a spigot with a parting tool using the callipers as a guide (see Fig 18.23). Check that the spigot will fit the bowl recess before shaping the pedestal. When turning the pedestal, leave a ¼in (6mm) flat surface next to the spigot on which the corresponding flat on the bowl can sit (see Fig 18.24). Turn this to a bead, followed by a V and then make a waist flowing into a substantial base which will visually and ergonomically support the bowl. The pedestal should not be too thick nor too thin; the precise width is a matter of judgement to achieve something aesthetically pleasing and well balanced.

Prepare the pedestal for colouring and then, using similar or contrasting dyes, colour the pedestal including the bottom, and when dry seal with sanding sealer (see Fig 18.25).

Fig 18.25
Dyeing the pedestal with colours complementary to those used on the bowl, and sealing with sanding sealer once dry.

Gilding the bowl

While the sealer is drying return to the bowl and with it either on or off the lathe apply your chosen colour of gilt cream to selected areas of the interior. It doesn't need to be all over – restricting its use often makes a piece appear more precious. Rub the cream with your finger

Above **Fig 18.26**
Applying gilt cream to specific areas of the bowl by rubbing it across the grain with a finger. This is the same application technique as that used for applying liming wax.

Above right **Fig 18.27**
Removing surplus gilt cream from the work using Finishing oil.

across the grain, filling it in the same way as applying the liming wax (see Fig 18.26).

Allow the gilt cream to set hard. This should only require half an hour or so. The easiest way to remove the surplus from the stationary work is with Finishing or Danish oil on a piece of paper (see Fig 18.27). With care you can remove the surplus without spreading the cream to other areas of the bowl.

Finishing

When the thin film of oil has dried, apply neutral wax polish to the bowl, inside and out, and spin to polish. If the underside was difficult to reach and you are not satisfied with the finish, use the drill brush once more as described on page 109. Gild the pedestal in a similar manner (see Fig 18.28).

As a final touch, gild the rim of the bowl. Remount it on the lathe, and with a small round-ended brush paint the rim carefully with red fontenay base, revolving the work towards you as you paint (see Fig 18.29). If the fontenay strays over the edge wipe it off immediately. The fontenay will fill the open grain of the wood and dry to a hard surface which can be rubbed very smooth with fine steel wool. Wipe the surface over before taking a clean brush and pot

(a)

(b)

(c)

Fig 18.28
(a) Filling the open grain of the pedestal with gilt cream, (b) removing excess gilt with finishing oil, and (c) giving the piece a final polish with neutral wax polish.

Left **Fig 18.29**
Using a small round-ended brush to apply red fontenay base to the rim.

Fig 18.30
Applying a coat of gilt varnish to the dry, finished fontenay base.

of gilt varnish to match the gilt cream used on the bowl, and using the technique described on page 174, apply a coat cleanly and neatly over the fontenay or for added dimension allow the fontenay to peep through (see Fig 18.30). If the coverage is not as complete as you would like, wait until the gilt varnish is dry and apply a second coat.

Finally, using a suitable wood glue – I use PVA – marry the bowl and pedestal together (remembering to line up the grain) and you will have a piece of work which will not only please, but one which will bring home to anyone the possibilities of elevating wood into the realms of art (see Fig 18.31).

Fig 18.31
The finished piece accompanied by the peacock feather which provided the original inspiration for the colour scheme.

About
the author

After ten years as a successful professional willow basket maker, Jan Sanders developed her woodturning skills under the guidance of her husband John, a respected teacher of the craft. For the past six years she has been pioneering the enhancement of turned wood with the application of spectrum-colour dyes and stains. In 1994, after ten years as a full-time woodturner, Jan launched a video on the subject of colouring turned wood, sponsored by Liberon Waxes.

Jan Sanders is an inspiring demonstrator of turning and colouring at the major national woodworking shows, and at seminars across the UK and in Ireland. In 1992 she was elected to The Worshipful Company of Turners' Professional Register, and is a past vice-chairman of the Association of Woodturners of Great Britain. Jan is a founder member of the Wessex Woodturners Association and of Makers Contemporary Craft Co-operative in Taunton, where her work can be seen.

Jan Sanders, Potters Cottage, Northay, Chard, Somerset.

Metric conversion table

Inches to millimetres and centimetres

MM = millimetres   CM = centimetres

Inches	MM	CM	Inches	CM	Inches	CM
⅛	3	0.3	9	22.9	30	76.2
¼	6	0.6	10	25.4	31	78.7
⅜	10	1.0	11	27.9	32	81.3
½	13	1.3	12	30.5	33	83.8
⅝	16	1.6	13	33.0	34	86.4
¾	19	1.9	14	35.6	35	88.9
⅞	22	2.2	15	38.1	36	91.4
1	25	2.5	16	40.6	37	94.0
1¼	32	3.2	17	43.2	38	96.5
1½	38	3.8	18	45.7	39	99.1
1¾	44	4.4	19	48.3	40	101.6
2	51	5.1	20	50.8	41	104.1
2½	64	6.4	21	53.3	42	106.7
3	76	7.6	22	55.9	43	109.2
3½	89	8.9	23	58.4	44	111.8
4	102	10.2	24	61.0	45	114.3
4½	114	11.4	25	63.5	46	116.8
5	127	12.7	26	66.0	47	119.4
6	152	15.2	27	68.6	48	121.9
7	178	17.8	28	71.1	49	124.5
8	203	20.3	29	73.7	50	127.0

Index

TITLES AVAILABLE FROM
GMC Publications
BOOKS

WOODCARVING

The Art of the Woodcarver	*GMC Publications*
Carving Architectural Detail in Wood:	
The Classical Tradition	*Frederick Wilbur*
Carving Birds & Beasts	*GMC Publications*
Carving Nature: Wildlife Studies in Wood	
	Frank Fox-Wilson
Carving Realistic Birds	*David Tippey*
Decorative Woodcarving	*Jeremy Williams*
Elements of Woodcarving	*Chris Pye*
Essential Tips for Woodcarvers	*GMC Publications*
Essential Woodcarving Techniques	*Dick Onians*
Further Useful Tips for Woodcarvers	*GMC Publications*
Lettercarving in Wood: A Practical Course	*Chris Pye*
Making & Using Working Drawings for Realistic	
Model Animals	*Basil F. Fordham*
Power Tools for Woodcarving	*David Tippey*

Practical Tips for Turners & Carvers	*GMC Publications*
Relief Carving in Wood: A Practical Introduction	
	Chris Pye
Understanding Woodcarving	*GMC Publications*
Understanding Woodcarving in the Round	
	GMC Publications
Useful Techniques for Woodcarvers	*GMC Publications*
Wildfowl Carving – Volume 1	*Jim Pearce*
Wildfowl Carving – Volume 2	*Jim Pearce*
Woodcarving: A Complete Course	*Ron Butterfield*
Woodcarving: A Foundation Course	*Zoë Gertner*
Woodcarving for Beginners	*GMC Publications*
Woodcarving Tools & Equipment Test Reports	
	GMC Publications
Woodcarving Tools, Materials & Equipment	*Chris Pye*

WOODTURNING

Adventures in Woodturning	*David Springett*
Bert Marsh: Woodturner	*Bert Marsh*
Bowl Turning Techniques Masterclass	*Tony Boase*
Colouring Techniques for Woodturners	*Jan Sanders*
Contemporary Turned Wood: New Perspectives in a Rich	
Tradition	*Ray Leier, Jan Peters & Kevin Wallace*
The Craftsman Woodturner	*Peter Child*
Decorative Techniques for Woodturners	*Hilary Bowen*
Fun at the Lathe	*R.C. Bell*
Further Useful Tips for Woodturners	*GMC Publications*
Illustrated Woodturning Techniques	*John Hunnex*
Intermediate Woodturning Projects	*GMC Publications*
Keith Rowley's Woodturning Projects	*Keith Rowley*
Practical Tips for Turners & Carvers	*GMC Publications*
Turning Green Wood	*Michael O'Donnell*
Turning Miniatures in Wood	*John Sainsbury*
Turning Pens and Pencils	
	Kip Christensen & Rex Burningham

Understanding Woodturning	*Ann & Bob Phillips*
Useful Techniques for Woodturners	*GMC Publications*
Useful Woodturning Projects	*GMC Publications*
Woodturning: Bowls, Platters, Hollow Forms, Vases,	
Vessels, Bottles, Flasks, Tankards, Plates	
	GMC Publications
Woodturning: A Foundation Course (New Edition)	
	Keith Rowley
Woodturning: A Fresh Approach	*Robert Chapman*
Woodturning: An Individual Approach	*Dave Regester*
Woodturning: A Source Book of Shapes	*John Hunnex*
Woodturning Jewellery	*Hilary Bowen*
Woodturning Masterclass	*Tony Boase*
Woodturning Techniques	*GMC Publications*
Woodturning Tools & Equipment Test Reports	
	GMC Publications
Woodturning Wizardry	*David Springett*

WOODWORKING

Bird Boxes and Feeders for the Garden	*Dave Mackenzie*
Complete Woodfinishing	*Ian Hosker*
David Charlesworth's Furniture-Making Techniques	
	David Charlesworth
Furniture & Cabinetmaking Projects	*GMC Publications*
Furniture-Making Projects for the Wood Craftsman	
	GMC Publications
Furniture-Making Techniques for the Wood Craftsman	
	GMC Publications
Furniture Projects	*Rod Wales*
Furniture Restoration (Practical Crafts)	
	Kevin Jan Bonner
Furniture Restoration and Repair for Beginners	
	Kevin Jan Bonner
Furniture Restoration Workshop	*Kevin Jan Bonner*
Green Woodwork	*Mike Abbott*
Kevin Ley's Furniture Projects	*Kevin Ley*
Making & Modifying Woodworking Tools	*Jim Kingshott*
Making Chairs and Tables	*GMC Publications*
Making Classic English Furniture	*Paul Richardson*
Making Little Boxes from Wood	*John Bennett*
Making Shaker Furniture	*Barry Jackson*
Making Woodwork Aids and Devices	*Robert Wearing*

Minidrill: Fifteen Projects	*John Everett*
Pine Furniture Projects for the Home	*Dave Mackenzie*
Practical Scrollsaw Patterns	*John Everett*
Router Magic: Jigs, Fixtures and Tricks to	
Unleash your Router's Full Potential	*Bill Hylton*
Routing for Beginners	*Anthony Bailey*
The Scrollsaw: Twenty Projects	*John Everett*
Sharpening: The Complete Guide	*Jim Kingshott*
Sharpening Pocket Reference Book	*Jim Kingshott*
Simple Scrollsaw Projects	*GMC Publications*
Space-Saving Furniture Projects	*Dave Mackenzie*
Stickmaking: A Complete Course	
	Andrew Jones & Clive George
Stickmaking Handbook	*Andrew Jones & Clive George*
Test Reports: *The Router* and *Furniture &*	
Cabinetmaking	*GMC Publications*
Veneering: A Complete Course	*Ian Hosker*
Woodfinishing Handbook (Practical Crafts)	*Ian Hosker*
Woodworking with the Router: Professional	
Router Techniques any Woodworker can Use	
	Bill Hylton & Fred Matlack
The Workshop	*Jim Kingshott*

GARDENING

Auriculas for Everyone: How to Grow and Show
  Perfect Plants   *Mary Robinson*
Bird Boxes and Feeders for the Garden   *Dave Mackenzie*
The Birdwatcher's Garden   *Hazel & Pamela Johnson*
Broad-Leaved Evergreens   *Stephen G. Haw*
Companions to Clematis: Growing Clematis with
  Other Plants   *Marigold Badcock*
Creating Contrast with Dark Plants   *Freya Martin*

Gardening with Wild Plants   *Julian Slatcher*
Hardy Perennials: A Beginner's Guide   *Eric Sawford*
The Living Tropical Greenhouse: Creating a Haven
  for Butterflies   *John & Maureen Tampion*
Orchids are Easy: A Beginner's Guide to their Care
  and Cultivation   *Tom Gilland*
Plants that Span the Seasons   *Roger Wilson*

VIDEOS

Drop-in and Pinstuffed Seats   *David James*
Stuffover Upholstery   *David James*
Elliptical Turning   *David Springett*
Woodturning Wizardry   *David Springett*
Turning Between Centres: The Basics   *Dennis White*
Turning Bowls   *Dennis White*
Boxes, Goblets and Screw Threads   *Dennis White*
Novelties and Projects   *Dennis White*
Classic Profiles   *Dennis White*

Twists and Advanced Turning   *Dennis White*
Sharpening the Professional Way   *Jim Kingshott*
Sharpening Turning & Carving Tools   *Jim Kingshott*
Bowl Turning   *John Jordan*
Hollow Turning   *John Jordan*
Woodturning: A Foundation Course   *Keith Rowley*
Carving a Figure: The Female Form   *Ray Gonzalez*
The Router: A Beginner's Guide   *Alan Goodsell*
The Scroll Saw: A Beginner's Guide   *John Burke*

MAGAZINES

WOODTURNING ◆ WOODCARVING ◆ FURNITURE & CABINETMAKING
THE ROUTER ◆ WOODWORKING ◆ THE DOLLS' HOUSE MAGAZINE
WATER GARDENING ◆ EXOTIC GARDENING ◆ GARDEN CALENDAR
OUTDOOR PHOTOGRAPHY ◆ BUSINESSMATTERS

The above represents a selection of titles currently published or scheduled to be published.
All are available direct from the Publishers or through bookshops, newsagents and specialist retailers.
To place an order, or to obtain a complete catalogue, contact:

GMC Publications,
Castle Place, 166 High Street, Lewes,
East Sussex BN7 1XU, United Kingdom
Tel: 01273 488005 Fax: 01273 478606
E-mail: pubs@thegmcgroup.com

Orders by credit card are accepted